To:

From:

Date:

Moments with God
for Teen Girls

KAREN STUBBS

Christian art gifts®

Visit Christian Art Gifts, Inc., at www.christianartgifts.com.

Moments with God for Teen Girls: 100 Devotions

Published by Christian Art Gifts, Inc., IL, USA

Moments with God for Teen Girls © 2024 by Karen Stubbs. All rights reserved.

Designed by Alyssa Montalto

Cover and interior images used under license from Shutterstock.com.

Scripture quotations are taken from the *Holy Bible*, New Living Translation, copyright ©1996, 2004, 2015 by Tyndale House Foundation. Used by permission of Tyndale House Publishers, Carol Stream, Illinois 60188. All rights reserved.

ISBN 978-1-63952-466-2

Printed in China

29 28 27 26 25 24
10 9 8 7 6 5 4 3 2 1

DEDICATION

This book is dedicated to my three girls,
Kelsey, Emily, and Abby.
What a privilege to be your mom.

TABLE OF CONTENTS

A Message Just for You

Girls are near and dear to my heart. I come from a family of four girls, and I have three daughters of my own. I have mentored many young women through high school and college, and I feel like I know girls. I know your struggles, your insecurities, and your sometimes-fragile sense of worth. I also know the potential girls have in this world.

When my girls were in high school, they struggled finding the right devotional for them. Devotionals felt either too juvenile or too old. After starting my ministry for moms, Birds on a Wire, I kept hearing from moms of teenagers that their daughters were struggling in their walk with the Lord. I thought, Why not write a devotional just for teen girls? And so I did! I hope this devotional will be an encouragement to you and draw you closer to your heavenly Father who loves you dearly!

My hope and desire are that at the end of these next 100 days, you will know three things:

- YOU WERE CREATED FOR A PURPOSE.
- YOUR HEAVENLY FATHER LOVES YOU DEARLY, AND YOU ARE HIS CHILD.
- NO MATTER WHAT, GOD IS WITH YOU!

Love, Karen

You Are Not Too Young

Don't let anyone think less of you because you are young.
Be an example to all believers in what you say, in the
way you live, in your love, your faith, and your purity.
1 TIMOTHY 4:12

Don't ever feel like your opinion or thoughts don't matter because you are young. Even in your youth, what you think, feel, and believe is very important, especially to God. In the Bible, Timothy was chosen by Paul to be one of his missionaries, even though Timothy was considered to be very young for that job. The fact that Paul, a keystone figure in the early church who wrote most of the New Testament, chose Timothy to serve with him illustrates that youth doesn't matter in God's eyes. Timothy was a great helper to Paul and ended up being a great leader in the early days of the church despite his youth.

Like Timothy, God can use you despite your youth. You don't have to be a certain age to be "an example to all believers" and show God's love to others. You can be a good example to your friends at school, to your teammates, to the kids in your church youth group, and to the people you spend time with at your clubs, hobbies, and job. How are you to be a good example? Lead out in your speech, making sure your words are kind and full of love, not putting others down. Be an example in the way you live and love others, always treating everyone with respect and showing kindness to everyone, even the people outside of your friend group. Be an example in your faith, which means you don't always have to have the answers, but you do need to be transparent and show others that while you don't know everything, you are eager to learn. And lastly, be an example in your purity, putting God first and realizing your body and mind are the home of Jesus and the Holy Spirit.

Father,

Thank you that my age is not a factor with you. I love that
you "see" me and that you have a plan for my life. Give me
wisdom about how I can be a good example to everyone I come
into contact with. Guide me through every step of my life. I pray
that my life will make a difference, even as a teenager. Amen.

REFLECTION QUESTIONS

1. What are some times when you have felt like you're too young to make an impact on this world? What does the Bible say about being "too young"?

2. In the New Testament, Timothy says not to let your age stop you from living for God. How does this encourage you to start living for God and becoming a good example?

3. In what area of your life do you feel that God is calling you to be a good example? How can you work on that this week?

My Prayer and Reflection

_____

_____

_____

_____

_____

_____

_____

_____

_____

_____

_____

_____

_____

_____

_____

_____

God Looks at the Heart

When they arrived, Samuel took one look at Eliab and thought,
"Surely this is the Lord's anointed!" But the Lord said to Samuel,
"Don't judge by his appearance or height, for I have rejected him.
The Lord doesn't see things the way you see them. People judge
by outward appearance, but the Lord looks at the heart."

1 SAMUEL 16:6-7

Have you ever assumed that you can't do something because you're too young or you don't have any experience? Those things might matter to people, but God looks at something else—your heart. In this passage of Scripture, the prophet Samuel has been sent to anoint the next king of Israel. Eliab was a son of Jesse, which is the family that God told Samuel the next king would come from. Samuel looked at Eliab and thought he would become king because he looked the part. But God said no. God actually chose the youngest son, David. That's because God was focused on what truly matters—a person's heart.

Age—and appearance—didn't matter. God saw David's heart even as a young boy. David was anointed king that day by Samuel, but he was not appointed king until twenty years later. David had to wait twenty years before he was able to become king, but he grew during his time of waiting. Be patient while you wait on God's plan to unfold in your life. God has a plan for each of us. Be faithful to him and his word in your time of waiting, and don't doubt him. He has you, and he wants the best for you. While you are waiting for your time to come, examine your heart. Ask God to show you the things that needs to be worked out. God will show you if you trust in him.

The world focuses solely on the outer appearance of men and women, but God does not. God focuses on what truly matters, and that is your heart.

Father,
Thank you that you don't look on the outward appearance like the
world does. I admit that at times I can struggle with feeling bad
about my looks and feeling like I do not measure up to others.
Please help change my heart to one filled with your love. Amen.

REFLECTION QUESTIONS

1. In today's social media-influenced world, how can it be difficult for you not to focus on your outward appearance?

2. How do you feel knowing that God looks at the heart of a person over their outside appearance?

3. Do you think that your youth holds you back from dreaming and achieving your goals in life? How could you incorporate God into your dreams for the future?

My Prayer and Reflection

_____

_____

_____

_____

_____

_____

_____

_____

_____

_____

_____

_____

_____

_____

_____

Trust God

Fearing people is a dangerous trap,
but trusting in the LORD means safety.
PROVERBS 29:25

Fear is a powerful emotion. When you're scared, you can feel out of control. During your teenage years, people can cause a lot of "fear" in your life. You fear what people will think of you, how they will treat you, what they will say about you. Have you ever been afraid of losing friends? Have you ever felt anxiety walking into a room where you don't know anyone and you don't know if anyone will talk to you? Have you ever feared that no one will truly accept you for who you are? Fear is REAL.

There *is* someone you can always trust, and that someone is God. God is your safety net, both in your teen years and throughout the rest of your life. Learn to lean into him. Learn to give him all of your fears and anxiety. He can handle the truth, and he actually already knows your situation.

Sometimes it's hard to recognize, but you *can* hear God's quiet voice in your life. Listening to him is how you deepen your faith in him. He is there for you always, and he understands all that you are going through in your life. When you lose a friend, he stays your friend. When you think you don't know anyone in the room, remember that you know God. When you feel different and like nobody accepts you, know that God loves you exactly the way you are. He wants to be your safety net. Let him. Take a step toward him today.

Father,

I am fearful of people. I feel like one text or post from
a certain group or person could mess up my entire life.
God, I want you to be my safety net, my safeguard. I truly
do not know how to trust a God I cannot see, but I do
believe that you love me and want the best for me.
Help me to start growing my relationship with you.
I look forward to our time together. Amen.

REFLECTION QUESTIONS

1. In what areas of your life do you find yourself being fearful?

2. Right now, what do you do when you feel that fear?

3. List a few ways you can start trusting God with your fear. (Example: *When I am fearful, I will ask God to give me courage.*)

My Prayer and Reflection

_____

_____

_____

_____

_____

_____

_____

_____

_____

_____

_____

_____

_____

_____

_____

_____

_____

Be Grateful

Don't worry about anything; instead, pray about everything. Tell God what you need, and thank him for all he has done. Then you will experience God's peace, which exceeds anything we can understand. His peace will guard your hearts and minds as you live in Christ Jesus.

PHILIPPIANS 4:6-7

How fortunate we all are that the God who created the universe wants to have a relationship with us. God wants to hear what is going on in our lives. He truly cares! Today, you can tell him exactly what is going on in your world. Talk to God about what your dreams are, how your relationships are doing, which classes you are struggling with and which ones you are enjoying. Tell God about all the things in your life you are worrying about. Let him know what your biggest worries are right now: people not accepting you, kids laughing at you, failing a test or an entire course, making mistakes in your sport, not being good enough to achieve something. Whatever your worries are, share them with God.

One way to work against worrying is to be grateful. Give thanks for the exact situation you find yourself in. When we worry, we are declaring that what we have and are doing is not enough. But when we take on an attitude of gratitude, there is no room left for "not enough" because we are declaring the good in our life. If you don't think you can find anything to be grateful for today, just thank God that he cares for you and wants to listen to your troubles.

Once you start practicing this mindset, you will start experiencing God's peace, which is like no other. Regardless of your situation, you are in God's very capable hands, and you can trust him.

Father,

Thank you for your love. It sounds so simple, yet it is life-changing. Help me to realize that when I have you by my side, I do not need to worry about anything. You are enough to get me through these hard years. My strength is in you. Thank you for listening to all of my concerns. It makes me feel better knowing you are there for me. Amen.

REFLECTION QUESTIONS

1. If you could choose not to be worried or anxious, how do you think would life look different for you?

2. What is one worry you would gladly turn over to God and be rid of? What do you think would happen if you eliminated this worry from your life?

3. How can you do a better job of trusting God?

My Prayer and Reflection

_____

_____

_____

_____

_____

_____

_____

_____

_____

_____

_____

_____

_____

_____

_____

_____

_____

_____

Have a Good Attitude

Even though the fig trees have no blossoms, and there are no grapes on the vines; even though the olive crop fails, and the fields lie empty and barren; even though the flocks die in the fields, and the cattle barns are empty, yet I will rejoice in the Lord! I will be joyful in the God of my salvation!
HABAKKUK 3:17-18

We are not promised nor guaranteed a life without hardship. Quite the opposite—some parts of your life will be hard, and things will not always go your way. So don't be surprised when this happens. Instead, be ready. When life starts treating you unfairly and it feels like everyone is against you, your attitude will be the game-changer. You can have a good attitude in hard times by keeping your eyes focused on God and remembering that he is your salvation. You can't always change the people or circumstances around you, but having a good attitude is always *your* choice.

God promises to provide a way for you, even during your darkest days. He is for you, not against you. God loves you more than you can ever imagine. He proved that by sending his Son, Jesus, to die for you. Thank God for that and realize there is nothing too big for God to handle. He may not work it out the way you think is right, but trust him. His way is always the best way. When you remember this, you can have a good attitude.

Father,

Open my eyes to see past my own circumstances in life and help me trust in you. Help me, Lord, to see that you truly work all things together for good (Romans 8:28). Sometimes in my life, I can't see that truth at all. Yet I know I need to trust you, so please teach me how to do that. I am willing, and I want to learn. Thank you for being patient with me. Amen.

REFLECTION QUESTIONS

1. In what ways do you think your life is less than perfect?

2. Why do you think a good attitude can make a difference in life?

3. What does it mean to you that God truly works all things together for good?

4. What are some of the good things you see him doing in your life?

My Prayer and Reflection

Be Humble

God blesses those who are humble,
for they will inherit the whole earth.
MATTHEW 5:5

The world we live in—especially the world of social media—is all about calling attention to yourself. It is forever shouting, "Look at me! See how amazing I am!" But God sees the world differently. He blesses those who are humble—those who *don't* call attention to themselves. God declares to us that he sees us, even when no one else is looking. He sees us when we feel invisible, and he promises to bless us. Always keep in mind, God's ways are not our ways. His wisdom usually seems countercultural. Like the wisdom of being humble.

Always choose a humble spirit. A spirit where you are not calling attention to yourself, telling others how great you are. Allow people to figure that out on their own. You are great! God says you are! But let your actions prove it, not your voice. It is better for other people to praise you than for you to praise yourself all the time. Think about it—you don't love being around someone who brags all the time, do you? It can get really annoying. God doesn't want us to be annoying. He doesn't want us to draw that kind of attention. He wants his children to be humble, and if we are humble, he will bless us beyond measure.

Father,

Thank you for loving me and teaching me your ways.
It's easy to be tempted to brag because I want people around
me to know that I am smart, I am talented, and I have something
to offer. When I am bragging, though, all I am doing is looking
for approval from others. Help me to realize and believe that all
I need in life is your approval, and I already have that. Amen.

REFLECTION QUESTIONS

1. Who or what comes to mind when you hear the word "humble"?

2. If you were to act out being humble in your life, what would that look like for you? Give three real-life examples. (For instance, what would it look like for you to be humble at school?)

3. In what area of your life do you think you would benefit from taking a posture of humbleness? How can you focus more on lifting up others instead of talking up yourself?

My Prayer and Reflection

_____

_____

_____

_____

_____

_____

_____

_____

_____

_____

_____

_____

_____

_____

_____

_____

_____

_____

Faith and Action

You say you have faith, for you believe that there is one God.
Good for you! Even the demons believe this, and they tremble in terror.
How foolish! Can't you see that faith without good deeds is useless?
JAMES 2:19-20

There is an old saying that goes, "Put your actions where your mouth is." This saying applies to being a Christian too. Don't just say you believe in Jesus—act it out in your life! The Bible tells us that faith without actions is useless. What this means is, don't just believe in Jesus; live it out in your life. Jesus was full of love toward everyone he encountered, and he showed them his love with actions. We should be the same way.

You can live out your faith by serving others, being respectful, treating others with kindness and love, and putting others' needs before your own. You can live out your faith with your friends, classmates, and even with people you don't know well. And you can also live out your faith with your own family. Have you ever thought about that? How do you treat your parents? Your siblings? If someone on the outside looked into your home, would they be able to see Jesus' love made evident in your relationship with your family?

If you never told anyone you were a Christian, would they be able to tell it on their own just by watching the way you live? Would they be able to see it by how you acted in school? By how you treated your teammates? By how you interacted with your peers? Put your actions where your mouth is—live out your faith.

Father,

I'm not sure I've ever put these two ideas together, that my faith and the way I live my life should line up. Give me the courage to live out my faith, not just to say I believe but to really live it out. I want people to be able to "see" you in my life. This way of living life is different and challenging for me, so please give me your courage and your strength. Amen.

REFLECTION QUESTIONS

1. How do you naturally show the love of Jesus to others in your life?

2. How are you good at doing this? What parts of this are hard for you?

3. Have you ever thought about "living out your faith"? What does this statement mean to you?

4. How can you do a better job of living out your faith this week at school? In church? At home with your family?

My Prayer and Reflection

_____

_____

_____

_____

_____

_____

_____

_____

_____

_____

_____

_____

_____

_____

_____

_____

_____

Care for Your Parents

Children, obey your parents because you
belong to the Lord, for this is the right thing to do.
EPHESIANS 6:1

In the Bible, God gives us promises. And in the Ten Commandments, God gives us a specific promise: *if* you honor your father and mother, things will go well for you and you will live a long life. That's a pretty good promise. The question is, what does honoring your father and mother look like? You can honor your parents in many different ways. You can be respectful to them and listen to what they have to say (that doesn't automatically mean you are agreeing with them, but you *are* listening). You can be loving in your tone and attitude toward them. Another way to honor your parents is to listen to their ideas and opinions. Once again, you don't always have to agree with them, but you *can* listen to what they have to say. When we choose to get along with others, we will live happier lives. This principle is true with our parents as well. When we live in harmony with others—like our parents, even when we're teenagers—our health will be better, our anxiety will be lower, and we will be more at peace.

There is a natural hierarchy in life concerning authority: God first, then parents, then children. God has put this hierarchy in place to protect you, even when you're a teenager. God has placed your parents in authority over you to protect you and keep you safe, even when you are getting close to being an adult. You parents will have to answer to God one day on how they managed being your parents, but in the meantime your job is to honor them. When you choose to obey what God is asking of you, he will in turn bless you.

Father,
Honoring my parents isn't always easy. Sometimes I don't agree with what they are telling me and I don't like it. But I want to obey what you have asked of me. I want to do what is right in your eyes, so I will choose to honor my parents. Give me the courage and strength to hold my tongue when I disagree with them and to love them regardless of how things are going between us. Thank you for your promise to me. Amen.

REFLECTION QUESTIONS

1. What makes it difficult for you to honor your father and mother?

2. How can you choose to still honor your parents even when you don't share the same ideas and opinions?

3. Dream for a moment. What would your household look like if you chose to respect your parents? Would your house be a happier place to come home to? How do you imagine everyone treating each other, and what kind of atmosphere would you have?

My Prayer and Reflection

_____

_____

_____

_____

_____

_____

_____

_____

_____

_____

_____

_____

_____

_____

_____

_____

_____

_____

Treat Everyone Equally

My dear brothers and sisters, how can you claim to have faith in our glorious Lord Jesus Christ if you favor some people over others?
JAMES 2:1

It is easy to favor one person over another. It is easy to gravitate toward certain personalities or to think that one group of friends is better than another. Truth is, everyone is equal in God's sight. When Jesus lives inside of you, his thoughts become your thoughts and his ways become your ways—and one of those ways is treating everyone the same. It is okay to have a "best friend." Even Jesus had his dear friends like Peter and John, but Jesus made sure that he treated *everyone* with the same compassion and love. Jesus was never prejudiced against a group of people that was different from him. Just the opposite—he met people where they were and loved them no matter what.

We need to act the same way. We need to treat others with love and respect, even if they are different than us and we don't feel like we can relate to them. All people are equal, even in a high school setting where people tend to divide themselves up into groups. Just remember that in Jesus' eyes, no one group is better than or worse than another group. Have the motto "love well" be part of your everyday life, and treat everyone equally.

Father,

Thank you for loving me and sending your Son, Jesus, to show me how to act in love toward others. It's easy for me to think that I am better or worse than another person, and I realize that is wrong. Forgive me for thinking that way. Open my eyes and help me to see people the way you see people—and to treat them equally with love and respect. Amen.

REFLECTION QUESTIONS

1. What does it mean to you to treat everyone equally?

2. How can you treat someone who is not your favorite person with love and respect? If someone has been mean to you, how can you still show them God's love while keeping yourself safe?

3. If you were to pray and ask God to open your eyes and allow you to see people the way he sees people, what do you think you would see?

⨳ My Prayer and Reflection ⨳

_____

_____

_____

_____

_____

_____

_____

_____

_____

_____

_____

_____

_____

_____

_____

_____

_____

God Cares for You

Understand, therefore, that the LORD your God is indeed God.
He is the faithful God who keeps his covenant for a
thousand generations and lavishes his unfailing love
on those who love him and obey his commands.
DEUTERONOMY 7:9

Do you know that you are dearly loved by God? He loves everything about you. He loves your strengths and your weaknesses. He loves your personality, your quirky ways, your sense of humor, and the way you embrace life. God cares for you so much, and he wants to lavish his great love on you. And he will if you let him.

We allow God to lavish his love on us when we obey him. Obedience is so important for those who love God. When you obey God, you are protected by him because you are under his umbrella. When you step outside of God's will, choosing your own way over his way, you step out from his umbrella of protection. Sometimes you may not feel God's love for you, but it is not because he doesn't love you—it is because you have disobeyed him and gone your own way. This can be easy to do when we're being influenced by others, trying to make our own decisions for the first time or just wanting to show our independence. When this happens, ask for forgiveness and get back in step with God. Always remember, no matter what you do or how far you run from God, he cares for you. He will always take you back in and lavish his great love on you!

Father,

Thank you for your love. It is hard for me to comprehend why you
love me so much. I sometimes feel like I am not worthy of your love,
but I am grateful. Help me to believe and trust in you. I want
to feel your great love for me. I want to follow you and obey you
in everything I do. Help me to forgive myself when I disobey and
when I mess up. I am thankful that you care for me, Lord. Amen.

REFLECTION QUESTIONS

1. Why does obeying God feel difficult sometimes? How has it gotten more difficult as you've gotten older?

2. When do you feel most worthy of God's love? When do you feel most unworthy?

3. What do you think it means to step back "under the umbrella" of God's love and protection through obedience? Can you remember a time when you've done this? What happened?

My Prayer and Reflection

_____

_____

_____

_____

_____

_____

_____

_____

_____

_____

_____

_____

_____

_____

_____

_____

Care for the Less Fortunate

Instead, invite the poor, the crippled, the lame, and the blind.
Then at the resurrection of the righteous, God will reward
you for inviting those who could not repay you.
LUKE 14:13-14

Get into a habit of seeing those around you that are less fortunate than you are. You may have to look hard at first to find someone outside of your friend zone, but those people are there. You may not be able to find the poor, crippled, lame, or blind people, but you will find people who are poor in spirit, people who are crippled by their own negative feelings about themselves, people who are struggling with anxiety or depression, and people who are blind to God's love for them. They're all around you, if you notice them. Learn how to reach out and love these people.

When you walk into the cafeteria of your school, stop for a moment and look around the room. Don't just focus on where your friend group sits, but look at all the people sitting in different spots. Can you find someone sitting by themselves? Do they sit alone every day? If yes, that could be someone you choose to be kind to and invite them to sit with you. Or you can just sit down with them. It might be hard at first, but it's what Jesus did. He cared for the less fortunate by first joining them and then showing them kindness and compassion.

Father,

Open my eyes to everyone around me and show me the world
that you see. I want to love like you love. It's easy to only focus on
myself, my friends, my world. But I am starting to realize that there
is a much bigger world out there, and that you love everyone in it.
Teach me—I am willing to learn and become more like you. Amen.

REFLECTION QUESTIONS

1. When you read about "the poor, the crippled, the blind, and the lame," what comes to mind? What do you think of when you hear the term "less fortunate"?

2. Who instantly pops into your mind when you imagine people you could minister to? Make a list of these people, and start treating them the way Jesus would treat them.

3. What are some specific ways you can minister to people less fortunate than you this week? Write down what happens, how they respond, and how you feel after you've spent time with them. What do you think God is teaching you? How is he changing your heart?

❧ My Prayer and Reflection ❧

_____

_____

_____

_____

_____

_____

_____

_____

_____

_____

_____

_____

_____

_____

_____

_____

God Comforts Those Who Mourn

God blesses those who mourn, for they will be comforted.
MATTHEW 5:4

Isn't it amazing that the same God who created everything in heaven and earth also cares about those who are sad and are grieving a loss? We grieve and mourn many things in our lives, not just the death of a person. Right now, you could be grieving the loss of a friendship, the end of your parents' marriage, the death of a beloved pet, the end of your first relationship, the loss of a longtime dream you've had for yourself. There are so many things in this life that bring us sadness and that we can count as a "loss."

Always remember that in the middle of your sadness, God cares. He cares for you and your sorrow, and he promises to comfort you. God's comfort goes beyond understanding. He may not change your circumstances, but he will carry you through them and get you safely to the other side. Believe that with all your heart. When you're mourning something—a person, a pet, a passion—let yourself be comforted by God.

Father,
Thank you for comforting me when I am deep in my grief.
Sometimes life can be so overwhelming. Thank you for always
being there for me, for caring for me and loving me. I am so
grateful for all that you are and all that you bring to my life. Amen.

REFLECTION QUESTIONS

1. God cares for you so deeply that he wants to comfort you when you are down. Write down some ways that you have experienced God caring for you in your life.

2. In what ways do you think he provides you comfort? How can you be like him and comfort someone else who is mourning something?

3. What loss have you experienced recently? How is God helping you with this situation?

My Prayer and Reflection

_____

_____

_____

_____

_____

_____

_____

_____

_____

_____

_____

_____

_____

_____

_____

_____

_____

The Holy Spirit Is Our Advocate

*And I will ask the Father, and he will give you
another Advocate, who will never leave you.*
JOHN 14:16

It's always nice to have an advocate. An advocate is someone who stands up for you, is on your side, and speaks for you when you can't find the right words. Jesus says in John 14:16 that he is asking his Father, God to give YOU such an advocate, and that person is the Holy Spirit. Many times we don't think about the Holy Spirit, and we don't really know what his purpose is in our lives. However, the Holy Spirit is a key member of the Trinity of God. The Holy Spirit is FOR you. He will be your advocate in life, and he will be on your side and speak to God for you.

There will be times in your life when you are so angry, sad, or emotional that you will not know how to pray to God, but the Holy Spirit can speak for you to God. In those times, you can ask the Holy Spirit to tell God exactly how you are feeling because the Holy Spirit will know the right words to say, even if you can't find them. The Holy Spirit, who lives inside of you as a Christian, is the key to the power of God. You can ask for the Holy Spirit to be with you daily, to teach you, to share his wisdom with you, and to comfort you in your time of pain. He is always, always there for you. Isn't it nice to know that even though you feel alone sometimes, you are truly never alone? God is with you through the Holy Spirit. He is your advocate.

Father,

*Thank you for your gift of the Holy Spirit and that he is my advocate.
I want to learn more about him, including how to walk after him. I thank
you that I am never alone, that you are always with me. That alone
brings me comfort because many times at school or even when I'm
in a group of friends, I feel very alone. It is nice to know that I am not.
Thank you that I always have a friend—and an advocate. Amen.*

REFLECTION QUESTIONS

1. Do you have an advocate in your life right now? Who are they? What impact do they have on your life?

2. What do you think it means that the Holy Spirit is speaking to God on your behalf?

3. How do you think the Holy Spirit being your advocate can change your life?

4. What do you want the Holy Spirit to communicate to God on your behalf?

 *My Prayer and Reflection*

_____

_____

_____

_____

_____

_____

_____

_____

_____

_____

_____

_____

_____

_____

_____

_____

_____

_____

_____

_____

Jesus Has Overcome

*I have told you all this so that you may have peace in me.
Here on earth you will have many trials and sorrows.
But take heart, because I have overcome the world.*
JOHN 16:33

Did life seem a lot easier when you were a little kid? Now that you're older, you've probably experienced some major hurts. A friendship or a relationship that ended. Being bullied. Family problems. Failure—in school, in sports, or in something else that means a lot to you. Sometimes as Christians we believe the lie that God will spare us from sorrow, from pain, from hurt of any kind. That belief can be devastating to you and your perception of God. If you believe that God will spare you from hardship, then when it happens, your view of God is destroyed.

Jesus tells us just the opposite. He says that we "will have many trials and sorrows." Jesus is letting us know that even though we are followers of God, we will not be spared—it is just part of living on this earth. But there's good news! Jesus has overcome the world, and he promises to get you through any trial, any hardship, or any sorrow. We just need to lean into him and ask him for his deliverance. Even when the world feels like everything in this world is working against you, Jesus has already overcome the world for you.

Father,
*Of course I do not want to have any bad things happen in my life,
but I know I will have to go through hardships. Thank you for Jesus.
Thank you that he overcame the world with his death on the cross.
Help me to keep my eyes on Jesus—especially during hard times. It is so
easy for me to fall into self-pity, but remind me to look to Jesus, because
he will always get me through, and he has already overcome. Amen.*

REFLECTION QUESTIONS

1. How does it make you feel when you hear "you will have many trials and sorrows"?

2. Jesus said, "I have overcome the world." How do you think Jesus overcoming the world over two thousand years ago affects your life today?

3. What are some things you're having trouble overcoming right now? How do you think Jesus can help you overcome these things?

My Prayer and Reflection

_____

_____

_____

_____

_____

_____

_____

_____

_____

_____

_____

_____

_____

_____

_____

_____

_____

_____

_____

Be Free of Guilt

*Finally, I confessed all my sins to you and stopped trying
to hide my guilt. I said to myself, "I will confess my rebellion
to the LORD." And you forgave me! All my guilt is gone*

PSALM 32:5

Have you ever done something and immediately felt guilty about it? Maybe you lied to your parents about who you hung out with. Maybe you treated someone unkindly just because everyone else did. Maybe you keep making bad choices but don't really know how to stop. Guilt can sit heavy on us all. It weighs us down, bringing shame on us. And that's not all. Guilt keeps us far from God or anyone who loves us, because we feel bad for our wrongful acts and our natural inclination is to avoid the person who's making us feel that guilt—even if they're not saying anything. The enemy wants you to feel guilt and shame, keeping you isolated and alone. But God wants the opposite for you. God wants you to know that your sin has already been forgiven by the death of Jesus on the cross.

God loves you so much that he sent his only Son, Jesus, to pay for all your sin. In Jesus, your sin is washed away and forgotten; all you need to do is to confess your sin before God. Go to God and let him know what you have done, whether it be gossiping, lying, stealing, being unloving toward people, sexually sinning, drinking, doing drugs—God already has forgiven your sin. Ask him for his forgiveness. When you confess your sin before God, all your guilt will be gone. What a wonderful feeling it is to be free of guilt. It is a huge gift from God, so accept it and be free!

Father,

*I almost can't believe that you would forgive all of my horrible sin. How
can that be true? I have a hard time forgiving someone who has said
something mean about me. Yet I am going to believe you, Lord, and I am
going to accept this amazing and underserved gift from you. I cannot
wrap my mind around your great love for me, but I am going to choose
to walk in faith. Help me to remember your love for me every day. Amen.*

REFLECTION QUESTIONS

1. How does guilt weigh you down?

2. Why do you think is it so hard to accept God's forgiveness? Do you not feel like you deserve it? Does it seem too good to be true? Why or why not?

3. Describe what a guilt-free life would look like to you. How would it change the way you live, act, and feel?

My Prayer and Reflection

_____

_____

_____

_____

_____

_____

_____

_____

_____

_____

_____

_____

_____

_____

_____

_____

Bring Your Complaints to God

*I cry out to the LORD; I plead for the LORD's mercy. I pour out
my complaints before him and tell him all my troubles.
When I am overwhelmed, you alone know the way I should turn.*
PSALM 142:1-3

Do you ever feel like no one is listening to you? Do you feel like no one understands the pressure that is on you, the social turbulence you experience every day, the feeling that you don't measure up and you are drowning in confusing emotions, impossible responsibilities, and just all-out stress at times?

God cares, and he wants to hear from you. Cry out to him—let it all out. Tell God about your friend troubles, school problems, parent issues, the pressures you face every day, and let him hear your heart. You can never talk to God too much. Beg him to give you wisdom and knowledge to know what to do, to determine the best way to handle situations. He will answer you. It may be through a trusted mentor, a teacher, a coach, or even through your parents. He may choose to minister to your heart through a certain Bible passage, song, or something in nature. God has many ways in which he reaches down and touches the lives of his children and lets you know he is there.

Don't worry about seeming like a whiner. God *wants* you to bring everything to him—even your complaints! Always know that you have someone who will listen to you and *wants* to listen you.

Father,

*Thank you for being there for me. Thank you that I can cry out to you,
that I can pour my heart out to you—the good, the bad, and the ugly—
and that you are there for me. I pray that I will learn to turn to you
on a more consistent basis. I am learning to trust you, God. Amen.*

REFLECTION QUESTIONS

1. Do you have anyone in your life who you feel truly listens to you? Who are they, and what do they mean to you?

2. How does it make you feel to know that God wants to listen to all of your complaints—your hurts, your sadness, and your anger?

3. Describe a time in your life where you felt God ministering to you. What happened? How did that make you feel?

 *My Prayer and Reflection*

_____

_____

_____

_____

_____

_____

_____

_____

_____

_____

_____

_____

_____

_____

_____

_____

_____

God Is Faithful

But if we confess our sins to him, he is faithful and just to forgive us our sins and to cleanse us from all wickedness.

1 JOHN 1:9

Confession is a difficult thing. When we confess, we are acknowledging our part in wrongdoing. Confession is humbling, and no one likes to humble themselves. Our natural reaction is to blame others for our own wrongdoing. It's hard to take the blame ourselves. It can make us look bad, and we tend to say things like, "They pushed me to do it"; "I couldn't say no"; or "I didn't realize what I was doing." But the truth is, no one makes us decide what we do. *We* are in control of that. However, when we confess what our sin is and we humble ourselves before God, he is faithful and promises to forgive us of our sin.

It's a good trade-off: confess your sins, and God cleanses you from all wrongdoing. Think about how much freer you will be with no weight holding you down or guilt keeping you isolated. God wants you to be carefree. He wants you to feel his love for you. It's hard to humble yourself. It's hard to take the blame. It's hard to admit that you made a mistake. But when you confess your sins, God is faithful to forgive you.

Father,

Thank you for your faithfulness to always forgive me for my sins. I guess pride keeps me from confessing my sins to you, but I want to push past that pride, because I want your freedom and love. I need to be courageous and cry out to you. You are there for me. Thank you that when I confess my sins, you will forgive me. Amen.

REFLECTION QUESTIONS

1. What is the hardest part of confession for you?

2. Why do you think it so hard for us to admit that what we did was wrong and take ownership of our actions?

3. How do you feel when you do confess and the other person forgives you and doesn't bring it up again? How do you feel when you do this with God?

ℰ My Prayer and Reflection ℰ

_____

_____

_____

_____

_____

_____

_____

_____

_____

_____

_____

_____

_____

_____

_____

_____

_____

_____

Be Strong and Courageous

This is my command—be strong and courageous! Do not be afraid or discouraged. For the LORD your God is with you wherever you go.
JOSHUA 1:9

Have you ever felt like God was asking you do something or say something, but you were too scared to do what he asked? Maybe you felt like taking action or speaking up would cost you a friendship, or that someone would get mad at you. When you're not sure how someone is going to respond to you, it's hard to be strong and courageous. In Joshua 1:9, the Israelites were fearful, and they needed Joshua to tell them what to do. They were fearful because God was asking them to go into the city of Jericho and take it over. Can you imagine? They had been wandering around the desert for forty years, and God said it was now time for them to take the land he had promised them. But in order to take the land, they would have to fight. Joshua was letting the Israelites know that they would not be alone in their fight. God was with them, and he would fight for them.

The same is true for you today. In a culture where every day can feel like a fight between good and evil, a fight to stand up for your values and morals, you are not alone. God is letting you know to be "strong and courageous, your Lord and God is with you wherever you go." You aren't so different from Joshua in the Old Testament. The Israelites won the battle of Jericho (Joshua 6), and you will have victory in your life too when your strength comes from God. Learn to trust God, lean into him, and be strong and courageous. No battle is too big for God.

Father,

I want to be strong and courageous! I want to trust that you will always be with me and fight for me. Teach me, Lord. It is amazing that this story from the Old Testament is still applicable to me today. Help me to always remember you are the same, yesterday, today, and tomorrow. You never change. Amen.

REFLECTION QUESTIONS

1. What are some things in your life that make you feel fearful of speaking up or taking action?

2. Do you find yourself in a battle right now? What kind of a battle? Do you feel like you have support, or do you feel alone in fighting this battle?

3. How does it bring you peace to know that God is with you and will fight for you?

∽ My Prayer and Reflection ∽

_____

_____

_____

_____

_____

_____

_____

_____

_____

_____

_____

_____

_____

_____

_____

_____

_____

_____

Take Care of Your Own Problems Before Criticizing Others

And why worry about a speck in your friend's eye when you have a log in your own? How can you think of saying to your friend, "Let me help you get rid of that speck in your eye," when you can't see past the log in your own eye? Hypocrite! First get rid of the log in your own eye; then you will see well enough to deal with the speck in your friend's eye.

MATTHEW 7:3–5

It is so easy to criticize what others are doing wrong. It is so easy to sit around and talk about how your peers messed up, how they are failing in school or sports, how their friendships and relationships are falling apart. It is easy to look at someone else's life and judge them for being on the wrong path, for making bad choices, or from falling away from God. But Jesus warns us against this behavior. Jesus tells each of us to focus on ourselves first, and when we get rid of all of the yuck in our life, then we can look to "help" others.

If you find yourself being critical of others, always seeing the bad in another person, that is a good sign to stop and examine yourself. Think about your own life, then pray and ask God, "What log is in my own eye?" When God reveals your own stuff to you, confess it to him and ask for his forgiveness. Self-examination is a lot harder than pointing out another person's flaws. Don't be a hypocrite, Jesus tells us. Take care of your own self before judging others.

Father,

Sometimes I can be critical of others. I guess I do that because it makes me feel better about myself. Now that I confess this to you, I see how terrible it is. Why does putting down another person make me feel better about myself? Forgive me, Lord. Help me to examine myself before finding fault in others. Amen.

REFLECTION QUESTIONS

1. In what areas do you find yourself being the most critical of other people?

2. How do you feel after you criticize other people? How does it make you feel about other people—and about yourself?

3. If you were to examine yourself, what would the "log" in your eye be?

My Prayer and Reflection

Harsh Criticism Is Harmful

But if you are always biting and devouring one another,
watch out! Beware of destroying one another.
GALATIANS 5:15

One of the main themes in Jesus' life was to love others. He emphasized this so many times while he was on earth with us. He was always encouraging his disciples and followers, telling them that love was above all the most important thing. Why is it, then, that love seems to be so difficult for us humans? Even when you try to love others, you don't always get love in return. You can be made fun of for being "too nice," or people think you are "too good," or if you are too nice, you must be fake. Many times, we can easily just give in and start treating others the way we are treated: backstabbing, gossiping, exaggerating the story about someone else to make ourselves look good.

The Bible warns us that this type of behavior destroys other people. Your words and actions have consequences, and they affect the way others feel. You don't want to ever be part of destroying another person's self-esteem or self-confidence. No, you want to love others, build them up, and encourage them, just like Jesus asked us to do. Make sure your life represents love toward others, even people who are not like you.

Father,

Help me to love others even when they are not loving toward me.
I cannot give this type of love without Jesus doing it through me.
When people are mean to me, I want to either shut down or
lash out. Help me to choose love instead. I know that is the
right way to respond—it is just hard. I need your help. Thank you
for loving me and sending your Son, Jesus, to teach me. Amen.

REFLECTION QUESTIONS

1. In your friend group, how does everyone treat each other? Loving each other, or every girl out for herself?

2. How do you feel about the way others treat you? Would you want to be treated that way?

3. What would it look like if you started treating people the way Jesus treated others? Would people in your world notice a difference?

My Prayer and Reflection

_____

_____

_____

_____

_____

_____

_____

_____

_____

_____

_____

_____

_____

_____

_____

_____

_____

Go to God with Confidence

*So let us come boldly to the throne of our gracious God.
There we will receive his mercy, and we will find
grace to help us when we need it most.*

HEBREWS 4:16

When you think of God, what thoughts comes to your mind? Do you feel he is distant or he doesn't really listen when you pray? Is it hard for you to imagine that God is interested in the problems and can't relate to the issues of a modern-day teen? So many times, we don't pray to God because we think he isn't interested in hearing from us and doesn't get what our lives are like. But the opposite is true. God truly wants a relationship with you. He gets you. He cares about your life and wants you to share your thoughts, dreams, and emotions with him. God wants to walk this journey of life with you.

When you pray, don't be timid or shy, or believe the lie that God doesn't care about you. No! Go boldly to his throne, trying to visualize it in your mind. The God of the Universe, the creator of all things, cares about you and wants to hear what is going on in your life. He is asking you to enter into a relationship with him. Go boldly because you are a child of God. Let your requests be known, and then listen for his voice. He might speak to you through another person, through a verse in the Bible, or through a message at your youth group. There are many ways God can speak to you. Don't be afraid of going to God. He won't reject you or turn his back on you. Go to him with confidence, and receive his mercy and grace.

Father,

*The more I learn about your love for me, the more I am humbled.
Thank you for giving me your mercy and grace. I feel like with
everyone in my life, I have to earn their love and respect,
but you love me unconditionally and that is wonderful. I don't
think I understand all of it just yet, but I am beginning to
see your deep love for me and I am so thankful. Amen.*

REFLECTION QUESTIONS

1. What do you think the throne of God looks like? Describe in detail how you imagine it.

2. Look up Revelation 4:2-1. This is a description of God's throne. How do the verses describe it?

3. How is your description and Revelation's description of God's throne different? How is it similar?

4. God tells us to come boldly before his throne to receive his mercy and grace. How does that make you feel?

∽ My Prayer and Reflection ∾

_____

_____

_____

_____

_____

_____

_____

_____

_____

_____

_____

_____

_____

_____

_____

_____

_____

God Created a Good World

Then God looked over all he had made, and he saw it was very good!
GENESIS 1:31

Sometimes it's hard to see any good in the world. The climate feels very unstable, there is war and fighting, power-hungry people and nations are trying to control each other, pandemics and other diseases seem very scary. And then if you focus closer to your own community, there are plenty of problems there too. Families are splitting up, there are nasty divorces, you hear constant arguments, and people are getting hurt all around you. Even in your own world, you see people your age getting away with cheating, being mean, and lying, and they're not getting in trouble. At times, it can be almost impossible to believe we live in a good world.

Keep in mind that this is not the way God first created the world. In the beginning, God created the heavens and the earth and it was all good. There was no sin in the world until Adam and Eve disobeyed God and ate the apple (Genesis 3). When they did that, sin entered the world, and it has stayed ever since. These facts are important to remember because God didn't cause the sin— humans chose it. The good news is, God has made a way for us to survive this earth, and that is through his Son, Jesus, who came to set us free from sin. God is a good God, and even though bad things happen in this world, he will make it "right" again. Until then, we need to trust him and trust that he is a good Father. If we keep our eyes on God in the good times and the bad, he promises to get us through this world.

Father,
Thank you that you are a good Father. Thank you that you did create a beautiful world in the beginning, and your plan was for it to be perfect. Help me to look past all the evil that surrounds me and focus on your perfect love and your Son, Jesus. Help me to keep my eyes focused on you and your plan for all eternity. Amen.

REFLECTION QUESTIONS

1. How do you feel when you look around and notice all of the problems in the world? What are some of the things that concern you the most?

2. How do you reconcile that God is good, and created a good and perfect world, now that sin is here and seems to be taking over?

3. Jesus is the solution until God makes the world perfect again. What do you think this means for your life? How can this help you have a better outlook on things?

∽ My Prayer and Reflection ∾

_____

_____

_____

_____

_____

_____

_____

_____

_____

_____

_____

_____

_____

_____

_____

Fight Your Enemy

*The serpent was the shrewdest of all the wild animals the Lord God
had made. One day he asked the woman, "Did God really say
you must not eat the fruit from any of the trees in the garden?"*
GENESIS 3:1

You have an enemy in your life. His name is Satan, and Jesus said he is the father of lies (John 8:44). While it's not nice to know that you have an enemy, it *is* important to know that you have someone working against you, because then you know how to fight him. The wonderful truth is, YOU have power over him in the name of Jesus. In order to defeat your enemy, you must know his tactics. He comes at you in a sly way, and he tries to confuse you by speaking lies to you. His devices are not new; they have been around since the beginning of time. Look at how he deceived Eve in the Garden of Eden. The serpent (Satan) said to Eve, "Did God *really* say…?" He placed doubt in Eve's mind, trying to confuse her. That is exactly what he will do to you.

The enemy likes to make you doubt the truth when he whispers in your ear, "Is this *really* a sin? Everyone is doing it—how bad can it be?" Listen up! God's Word is the same yesterday, today, and tomorrow; he does not change. If lying was a sin two thousand years ago, it is still a sin today. There is nothing to be confused about. Know your enemy, but also know you have power over him in Jesus!

Father,

*I really haven't ever thought about the fact that Satan tries to confuse
me. I pray that I will begin to notice when he is speaking lies to me,
and that I will learn to lean into Jesus on calling him out. Give me
the strength to do that. Thank you that you have given me a
way to defeat my enemy! I am so thankful I am not alone. Amen.*

REFLECTION QUESTIONS

1. How do you feel about having an enemy in this world?

2. What are some of the lies Satan has told you or is currently telling you?

3. Knowing you have power over Satan, in the name of Jesus, is a powerful gift God has given you. What does that look like for you in your daily life?

My Prayer and Reflection

_____

_____

_____

_____

_____

_____

_____

_____

_____

_____

_____

_____

_____

_____

_____

_____

_____

_____

_____

_____

A New Heaven and a New Earth

Then I saw a new heaven and a new earth, for the old heaven and the old earth had disappeared. And the sea was also gone. And I saw the holy city, the new Jerusalem, coming down from God out of heaven like a bride beautifully dressed for her husband. I heard a loud shout from the throne, saying, "Look, God's home is now among his people! He will live with them, and they will be his people. God himself will be with them. He will wipe every tear from their eyes, and there will be no more death or sorrow or crying or pain. All these things are gone forever."

REVELATION 21:1–4

Have you ever had the best gift to give to someone and you couldn't wait to give it? A gift you poured your heart and soul into making? A gift you knew that the receiver was going to be super excited to get? That is exactly the way God feels about giving us a new earth. God is anxiously awaiting the day when the old earth will be gone and a new, perfect earth will be here! There will be no more sorrow, no more death, no more crying or pain. The best part of all is that God will actually walk among us on this new earth. We no longer will have to wonder what he looks like; we'll be able to look at him. We'll actually be able to sit down and ask him our questions, and he will answer us. How glorious will that day be?

Until then we must wait. On the days where you feel like the entire world is against you, remember that a day is coming when all pain will be gone. You might wonder, "Why do we have to wait?" We have to wait because God wants to gather as many believers as he can, to give every person a chance to live in eternity with him. What a day that will be when God will live with us, and this world will be perfect!

Father,

Wow! I cannot imagine what the new earth will look like. I know you give a detailed description of it in Revelation, but it sounds so wonderful. Help me to be patient while I wait. Thank you that I will have the opportunity to live with you in eternity. You are a good God! I love you! Amen.

REFLECTION QUESTIONS

1. Are you a patient person, or do you find that it's hard to wait for things?

2. What do you think the new earth will be like? What features would you be sure to include in a perfect, new earth?

3. What excites you most about having a new earth and being able to live in it?

My Prayer and Reflection

_____

_____

_____

_____

_____

_____

_____

_____

_____

_____

_____

_____

_____

_____

_____

_____

_____

_____

God's Word Is a Lamp

Your word is a lamp to guide my feet and a light for my path.
PSALM 119:105

Have you ever had times in your life when you've felt lost and confused? When you just didn't know which direction to take or which choice to make, and when you asked people for advice, you just became even more confused? That feeling of confusion may have left you feeling anxious, fearful, and overwhelmed, which is not a great way to live. It can even make you feel more anxious and confused the next time you were faced with a decision.

David writes in the book of Psalms that God's word is the light which shows us the way. David was a shepherd boy who was anointed to be the second king of Israel. David had many seasons in his life where he felt lost and alone and didn't know what to do. In those times, he would turn to God, and God always guided him in the right direction. In this dark world, where it seems like you can never find a true answer, God will show you the way if you read his word, the Bible. If you're confused about where to start reading God's Word, start in the gospels—Matthew, Mark, Luke, or John—and read about the life of Jesus and what he preached. You can also start with Proverbs and read great wisdom, or start with Acts and see how the first church exploded in numbers after Jesus left this earth. The Bible gives us so much wisdom and guidance from God that can truly help us in our lives today. Before you read God's word, ask him to open your eyes and show you his truth that will light your way.

Father,

I admit that most of the time in my life, I do not know what I'm doing. I may seem like I have my act together and it might look like I know what I'm doing, but most of the time I am guessing and aiming in the dark. Thank you for giving me a light to guide my path. I need your help, though, in understanding the Bible, because sometimes it goes over my head. Thank you for giving me your guidance when I read your Word. Amen.

REFLECTION QUESTIONS

1. What are some times you have felt lost with no direction in your life?

2. How do you handle the "lost" feelings? What do you do? (cry, get angry, become frustrated, try to think about something else?)

3. What do you think it means for God to be your lamp and guide your path?

4. How can you better allow God to guide you when you feel lost?

∾ My Prayer and Reflection ∾

_____

_____

_____

_____

_____

_____

_____

_____

_____

_____

_____

_____

_____

_____

_____

_____

_____

_____

_____

Seek Advice

Intelligent people are always ready to learn.
Their ears are open for knowledge.
PROVERBS 18:15

Who do you go to for advice? Does an older sibling or a parent give you really good advice? Do you rely on your friends to help you make decisions? Do you seek out advice on social media? You can find ideas and opinions everywhere you turn, but wise people seek advice from other wise people, to grow their own knowledge. The more good information you gain about a certain topic, the more facts you have to make the best decision. But you need to choose wisely who you're getting the information from. Fortunately, there are wise people all around you for you to lean into while you are making some pretty big decisions.

You have your parents, your teachers, your coaches, your small group leaders at church, your counselors at school, and even your grandparents available to give you advice. Go and ask these people their opinion on what "next step" you are contemplating. Whether it is which person to date, which college to apply to or attend, how to get out of an unhealthy relationship, or how to deal with friend drama, open your ears so you can hear—and apply—their knowledge. Then, pray and tell God what you have learned and ask him what is the best thing for you to do. After that, wait on God's answer. It may come through open doors, or affirmation through loved ones, or it may just be a peace he gives you in your situation. Finally, make your decision and be confident in it.

Father,

I have a confession: sometimes it is hard for me to ask for advice.
To be honest, I don't want to hear other people's opinions; I just want to
do what I want to do. I also don't want to take the time to seek advice,
I want to make a decision...NOW. Help me to push my pride aside and
humble myself and ask wise people for their advice. I don't want to
be a know-it-all. I want to know what you would like me to do. Amen.

REFLECTION QUESTIONS

1. What kind of decisions are you making in this season of your life? How do you feel about making all these decisions?

2. What are the hardest decisions you are wrestling with right now?

3. Who are some good people you can seek out to gain advice from?

4. What do you think God is telling you about the decisions you are making now and will be making soon?

My Prayer and Reflection

_____

_____

_____

_____

_____

_____

_____

_____

_____

_____

_____

_____

_____

_____

_____

_____

_____

_____

Ask for Wisdom

*If you need wisdom, ask our generous God, and
he will give it to you. He will not rebuke you for asking.*

JAMES 1:5

This verse is one of the best promises in the Bible. The promise is simple: if you need wisdom, just ask and God will give it to you. Not only will he give it to you, he will give it to you without finding fault in you or lecturing you or giving you a hard time for asking. That is a win/win.

How many times in your life have you sat in your room, driven in your car, or walked the halls of your school and thought, "I do not know what to do in this situation"? If you aren't comfortable asking your parents or another trusted person in your life for their wisdom, ask God. He is generous and will give you wisdom. Ask God for all types of wisdom. You can ask him for advice about what type of classes to pick for your schedule, whether or not you should date a certain guy that you like, if you should be friends with certain group of people, if it's a good idea for you take that extra job outside of school. No matter what the situation is, seek him with all your heart. And then when he gives you the wisdom, act on it. A lot of the time God's wisdom is much different than what we think we should do, but trust him. Always keep in mind, God is for you and he wants the best for you.

Memorize James 1:5 and use it throughout your life. It will remind you that God's wisdom is always readily available to you.

Father,

*Thank you for your promise to give me wisdom. I also love the
idea that you will not find fault in me—thank you for that. I love
that I can come to you, lay out my heart to you, ask you for what
I need, and you will give me wisdom without telling me how
wrong I am. Thank you for being a good, good Father. Amen.*

REFLECTION QUESTIONS

1. In what areas in your life do you feel like you need wisdom right now?

2. What do you feel like God is telling you to do?

3. Why does it sometimes feel hard to ask God for his wisdom? Why do you think it is important to ask him for his wisdom?

My Prayer and Reflection

God Helps Those Who Feel Crushed

The Lord is close to the brokenhearted;
he rescues those whose spirits are crushed.
PSALM 34:18

Your teenage years can be lonely years. There are many times where you might feel invisible to those around you. Every teenager around you—including you—is trying to figure out "who" they are. You live in a sea of insecure people, all overwhelmed, all trying to figure it out. When people are insecure, they can lash out and tear others down to make themselves feel better. If you are the recipient of this behavior, it can leave you feeling brokenhearted and rejected.

Always remember, you are not alone. God is with you, and in the times where you are feeling lonely and crushed, he will rescue you. In those times, cry out to God. Let him know the pressures you are under, how you feel like an outcast, even with your friends. God wants to hear all about your struggles with loneliness because he loves you and his desire is to care for you. He may use a worship song to minister to your soul, a sunrise or sunset to show you how big he is, a friend to reach out via text to just say hi, or a family member to ask you how you are doing. Those are all ways God will minister to you. Be on the lookout for these messages from your heavenly Father! You are not alone, and you are deeply loved.

Father,
These teen years are hard. I try to make wise choices, but
sometimes I get made fun of and that doesn't feel good.
Sometimes, Lord, I don't do anything wrong. I am just not invited
to a party or not included and that hurts too. Sometimes I do find
myself isolated and alone, and I do feel like my spirit is being crushed.
Help me to remember that my hope is not in my friends but in you.
Thank you for never leaving me and always loving me. Amen.

REFLECTION QUESTIONS

1. How do insecure people act toward you? Why do think they act that way?

2. How does it make you feel when people are mean to you? How do you tend to handle those situations?

3. What would it look like to allow God to minister to you when people are cruel to you? How do you think you would treat others after allowing God to help you?

ꙮ My Prayer and Reflection ꙮ

_____

_____

_____

_____

_____

_____

_____

_____

_____

_____

_____

_____

_____

_____

_____

_____

_____

_____

_____

Help Others

*We should help others do what is right and build them
up in the Lord. For even Christ didn't live to please himself.*
ROMANS 15:2–3

Thinking of others instead of ourselves can be a very foreign concept. Our naturally mentality is to think first about ourselves and how certain situations will affect us. But what if you took a different approach to life? What if you began to think of others before yourself and looked for ways to encourage them and put them first? If you took that approach in your school, in your home, and at your different activities, after several months people would notice. They would most likely see you as a kind, thoughtful person. What they wouldn't necessarily know is that Jesus is the source of your kindness and thoughtfulness.

How cool would that be if you could love people the way Jesus loves you? Try it! Test it out and see if people start noticing. Give it three months. What will happen is that more and more, Jesus will start showing you other people and their needs and how best to love them. You could be Jesus' personal assistant, loving on people. There are so many people walking around you every day who need an encouraging word, a smile, a friendly "hello, how are you today?" It doesn't take much to love and help others.

Father,

*Open my eyes and help me to "see" others around me in the
same way you see them. I do think about myself first most of
the time, and I would like to change that about myself. Teach me;
I want to learn. I want to love people the way you love me. Amen.*

REFLECTION QUESTIONS

1. Can you think of three people who would benefit from a little encouragement from you? Who are they?
2. What can you do this week to show these people some love?
3. What does "Love people the way Jesus loves you" mean to you?

My Prayer and Reflection

_____

_____

_____

_____

_____

_____

_____

_____

_____

_____

_____

_____

_____

_____

_____

_____

_____

_____

_____

_____

DAY 30 — *Encourage Others*

*Let us think of ways to motivate one
another to acts of love and good works.*
HEBREWS 10:24

Even if you never told anyone you were a follower of Christ, could they figure it out? Do you act like all of your peers, or are you different? Do you love others well? Sometimes it's hard to tell from our own perspective. We think we are loving others well, but actually we are doing the bare minimum. But a Christian should be known by their acts of love and good works toward others. And one of the best—and easiest—ways to show God's love is to encourage other people.

Today, take a survey of those who are the closest to you. Ask your parents, your best friend, or a favorite teacher or coach the following question: "Do you consider me to be a loving person to those around me?" Follow up that question with another question: "Can you think of some ways I could love others better?" Try not to be defensive when you hear their answers, but listen with open ears and an open heart. There is room for improvement for everyone. You want to be seen as someone who loves and encourages others well, someone who always points people toward their loving heavenly Father. With God's help, you can be that person.

Father,
Thank you for encouraging me to do what is right in loving others.
I love this verse in Hebrews, and I want to follow it. God, show me
ways I can love others well. I know I am selfish in my nature,
but with you helping me, I know that together we can love
others well. Thank you for never giving up on me! Amen.

REFLECTION QUESTIONS

1. Does the thought of "loving others" scare you a little bit? Why or why not?

2. If you were to push past your fear and love others well, what would that look like?

3. What do you have to lose by loving others?

4. What do you think it means to "motivate one another to acts of love and good works"?

My Prayer and Reflection

_____

_____

_____

_____

_____

_____

_____

_____

_____

_____

_____

_____

_____

_____

_____

_____

_____

_____

Faith Saves

So we are made right with God through
faith and not by obeying the law.
ROMANS 3:28

Rules, rules, rules—you are surrounded by them, day and night. Your parents have rules for you, your school has rules you must follow, the government has rules, even your friendships have certain unspoken rules. Did you know that God loves you even when you break his rules? God sent his Son to bear the full punishment of all the times you've broken his rules. He knows that if you have a heart for him and if you place your faith in him, then you will want to obey him from the heart. Following God is not about obeying all the rules and getting everything right all the time; it's about putting your faith in him, trusting his forgiveness for you, and walking with him.

Do you trust God and his Word? Do you believe that he loves you more than you can ever imagine and saved you from a life of death to give you life in Jesus? Once you truly accept Jesus as your Lord and Savior and follow after him with all your heart, he will empower you to walk with him. Holiness will come easier because you will be focused on pleasing Jesus, out of gratitude for what he did on the cross for you. We are made right with God, not by obeying the rules but by believing in Jesus. Jesus is enough! Jesus is the way. God knows that we can never obey every law and that we will never be perfect, so he made it easy for us. Follow Jesus. He is enough. Rules don't save us—faith does.

Father,

I feel like I'm bombarded by rules all the time, and I feel like half the time I am failing. What a relief to find out that I am saved by faith. Thank you for loving me despite me not always doing everything right. Help me to focus on Jesus and to start living my life the way he lived his life: loving others and being dedicated to you. Amen.

REFLECTION QUESTIONS

1. How do rules make you feel? Are you more of a rule follower or a rule-breaker?

2. What do you think about the idea that God is more interested in obeying him from a heart of love than out of duty?

3. What does following Jesus look like in your life right now? What are some ways you are following him?

My Prayer and Reflection

_____

_____

_____

_____

_____

_____

_____

_____

_____

_____

_____

_____

_____

_____

_____

_____

_____

_____

_____

_____

_____

Faith Brings Joy

Therefore, since we have been made right in God's sight by faith,
we have peace with God because of what Jesus Christ our Lord
has done for us. Because of our faith, Christ has brought us into
this place of undeserved privilege where we now stand, and we
confidently and joyfully look forward to sharing God's glory.
ROMAN 5:1-2

When we accept Jesus as our Lord and Savior, we are instantly placed in right standing with God. This placement is not because we have done everything right; just the opposite—it is because we have placed our trust in Jesus and not in ourselves. What an exchange! Because of Jesus, we can confidently and joyfully go before God with our prayers and share our heart with him—all of our burdens, dreams, and desires—and he will listen. He listens because he cares. God doesn't see all of our sin when he looks at us; instead, he sees his Son, Jesus. Knowing this should give us so much joy!

We live in a world where people can be pretty selfish. Even our friends can sometimes focus on themselves and not have an others-first mentality. Because of this, it can be hard for us in our human minds to wrap our brain around God's generous gift. Yet he gives us the gift of complete peace with almighty God, which is totally undeserved on our part. You are a child of God and have all the privileges that go with that title. When the enemy comes to try and destroy you by reminding you of everything you have done wrong, fight back. Remind him that you are a child of God and that you share in all of God's glory because of Jesus. And remember that your faith will always bring you joy!

Father,

Thank you for your gift of salvation in Jesus and that
I am at peace with you. Even though I have a hard time
comprehending such generosity, I choose to accept it.
Thank you for your Son, Jesus, who made this exchange
possible with his death on the cross. This type of unconditional
love is inspirational to me, and I want to joyfully accept it. Amen.

REFLECTION QUESTIONS

1. What do you think it means to be "made right" in the eyes of God? How does knowing that you have been made right impact your life?

2. What kind of privileges do you get for being a child of God?

3. Is it hard for you to accept such a gift? Why or why not?

My Prayer and Reflection

_____

_____

_____

_____

_____

_____

_____

_____

_____

_____

_____

_____

_____

_____

_____

_____

_____

_____

_____

_____

_____

Faith Has Two Parts

It was by faith that Abraham obeyed when God called him to leave home and go to another land that God would give him as his inheritance. He went without knowing where he was going.
HEBREWS 11:8

Are you learning to drive right now? Or have you recently learned how to drive? When you get behind the wheel of a car, you need to trust that the car is capable of getting you from point A to point B. But in order to actually change locations, you have to first put the keys in the car and start the engine, then put the car in drive and press the gas pedal. Just believing that the car can do it isn't enough. Action is required on your part. In a similar way, faith has two parts to it. The first part is trusting, and the second part is "doing"—or taking a step of action.

It is the same principle with God. It is wonderful to believe God and his Word. But we don't need to just believe, we need to act on that belief. God expects us to live out our faith through action, and he gives us many opportunities to do this—with our friend group, at our church, by volunteering, even when we're spending time at home with our families. In the Bible, Abraham believed God had an inheritance of a great land for him, so he acted on it. He packed up everything he had and moved to his new land. That is faith—believing *and* acting on it. We need both parts for our faith to work.

Father,

I will admit that sometimes I fall short on the two-step process of faith. I believe but I stop there, and I don't act on it. Stepping out in faith when I can't see the future is scary for me. Please give me the courage I need to do both. I want to follow you and trust you with all my heart. Amen.

REFLECTION QUESTIONS

1. What situations do you find it hard to trust God with?

2. What are some things you can do to build your trust in God?

3. The first part of faith is trusting and the second is doing, or taking a step of action. What do you feel God is calling you to do today? What makes it hard for you to take that step?

4. How can you trust God this week and take a step of action toward him?

My Prayer and Reflection

_____

_____

_____

_____

_____

_____

_____

_____

_____

_____

_____

_____

_____

_____

_____

_____

_____

Be Faithful

*If you are faithful in little things, you will be faithful
in large ones. But if you are dishonest in little things,
you won't be honest with greater responsibilities.*
LUKE 16:10

No matter how old we are or what's going on in our lives, many of us struggle in our faith. It is hard to trust a God we cannot see, to believe stories in the Bible that are thousands of years old. It is hard to believe that God is for us and not against us when everyone in our life seems to have unrealistic expectations of how we are supposed to act and perform. How can we build a strong faith with so many variables against us? Faith starts with trusting God, and then action is required to build your faith. Faith is like a muscle in your body—you can grow it. You can start small, just believing that God is who he says he is. Then pray and ask God to build your faith a little bit at a time. Ask God to reveal himself to you in a real, undeniable way.

In a world that stresses perfection, it is a relief that God does not require us to be perfect to have a relationship with him. Just the opposite—he asks that we as imperfect people believe in him, have faith that he is who he says he is, and then act on that faith by walking with him. God knows that no one can be perfect and obey the law 100 percent of the time—that would be impossible! He gave us another way, a better way, and that is to trust in him.

You don't have to start off with a huge amount of faith; you can start small. God will grow your faith muscle over time. Be faithful in the little things, and then he will give you more. Be honest and true to yourself in the small stuff, and God will bless you more as you grow. Be faithful.

Father,

*Please grow my faith like you would grow a plant in the woods.
My faith right now is fragile, but I do believe you are who you
say you are. I believe that you love me and want the best for me.
Sometimes I have a hard time trusting you with everything
in my life even though I want to. Give me courage to push
past my fear and trust you even though I cannot see you.
Reveal yourself to me in my life in real ways. Build my faith. Amen.*

REFLECTION QUESTIONS

1. On a scale of 1–10, with 1 being the weakest and 10 the strongest, what score would you give your faith? Why?

2. If faith is like a muscle and can become stronger, what is standing in the way of you taking that next step to grow your faith?

3. What is one area in your life where you could trust God more?

4. What are a few things you can do this week to strengthen your faith in God?

My Prayer and Reflection

_____

_____

_____

_____

_____

_____

_____

_____

_____

_____

_____

_____

_____

_____

_____

_____

_____

Do Not Fear

The Lord is my light and my salvation—so why should I be afraid? The Lord is my fortress, protecting me from danger, so why should I tremble?

PSALM 27:1-2

What if you were famous and had a bodyguard with you at all times? Someone who would protect you from your enemies, someone whose only job was to look after you? What if you were so famous that you had a public relations person who was constantly "righting" any offense that had been made against you? This PR person's only job was to watch out for your reputation and to make you look the very best you could look.

Did you know that we have something better than a bodyguard, better than a PR person? We have the almighty God, the creator of the Universe, who looks after us. We have the one true God who spoke life into this whole world. If he is on our side, how can we be afraid? And what could we possibly be afraid of in this world? There is nothing too big that God cannot handle. God wants to protect us from harm. He wants to "right" any offense that is made against us. He is on our side! Trust God. He will protect you from danger if you cry out to him and ask him for his help.

Father,

I pray that I would look to you always, whether I am afraid or whether I am having a great day. Teach me how to lean into you. It is my human nature to try and fix things on my own. I want to change that. I want to depend on you for everything because you are my protector and my strength. Amen.

REFLECTION QUESTIONS

1. What are you afraid of in your life? Which of your fears do you feel are too big for God to overcome?

2. What is one small step you could take this week toward trusting God more with your fears?

3. What do you think your life would look like if you didn't have any fear controlling it?

My Prayer and Reflection

_____

_____

_____

_____

_____

_____

_____

_____

_____

_____

_____

_____

_____

_____

_____

_____

_____

_____

_____

God is Our Refuge

God is our refuge and strength, always ready to help in times of trouble. So we will not fear when earthquakes come and the mountains crumble into the sea. Let the oceans roar and foam. Let the mountains tremble as the waters surge!

PSALM 46:1–3

In times of trouble, who do you talk to or text? Is it your friends, your small group leader, your coach, your mentor, your parents? We all find ourselves fearful at times in our lives, so it's important to know who we can reach out to for help. Talking to other people is important, but the best person we can talk to is God. Most of us don't think about calling out to God. God feels distant, he feels super big, and it seems like he won't have time for us, but the opposite is true.

God is our safe place who offers us shelter and strength. He is ready and willing to help us in any situation—big or small—if we just cry out to him. Talk to him as you would talk to your best friend. Let God know what is going on in your life, and why you are fearful. With God on our side, we truly have nothing to fear. There is no problem too big for him, no mountain too high. Remember who God is. His creations range from the smallest atom to the largest ocean and everything in between. He can handle your situation. God is your refuge, and with him on your side, there is nothing to fear.

Father,

The next time I am fearful, I am going to call out to you first. If I forget, will you gently remind me that you are there for me? My natural "go-to" is someone other than you, and I'm not really sure why—maybe because I can see them. But I do trust you, and I want to be dependent on you. Teach me how to trust you, especially in times of trouble. Amen.

REFLECTION QUESTIONS

1. Who is your go-to person you reach out to when you're stressed or anxious? Why do you go to them?

2. We go to certain people when we are in trouble because we trust them and they are safe for us. Do you feel like you can trust God? Do you feel like he is safe for you to take your troubles to? Why or why not?

3. Do you think there is a situation that God cannot handle? If so, describe what it is.

4. How do you think God can meet you where you are and help you in your time of need?

My Prayer and Reflection

_____

_____

_____

_____

_____

_____

_____

_____

_____

_____

_____

_____

_____

_____

_____

_____

Be Confident

*They do not fear bad news; they confidently trust
the Lord to care for them. They are confident
and fearless and can face their foes triumphantly.*
PSALM 112:7-8

Where do you place your security? Is it in your grades and in your identity as a smart person? Is it in your athletic skills or your abilities and talents as a dancer, a musician, an actor, or an artist? Do you gain security from the wealth of your parents and your status in society? Or does your friend group bring you security and confidence? None of those things are bad, but at any time they could be stripped from you, for various reasons. You could have an injury and have to sit out your sports or dance season. You could be rejected from the college of your choice or put on its wait list. Your friends could turn on you for no reason. You may not get the lead role in your play or concert. Where will your security come from if these things happen? What will happen to your confidence?

When we place our trust and confidence in worldly things, we will always be disappointed, but when we trust in God, our confidence will never lack. When or if bad news comes, we can accept it when our trust is in God, because we know he has a plan for us that is not based on our performance. We know that God wants the best for us, and he works all things together for our good (Romans 8:28). So be confident. Don't fear problems or setbacks in your life. Instead, be triumphant in your life and walk securely with God.

Father,

*Thank you that I have you on my side—always! So many times in my
life, I feel less than and insecure. But in you, I can be confident and have
victory over any fear that I face. Thank you for always going before me,
especially during the hard times. In you I place my trust. Amen.*

REFLECTION QUESTIONS

1. What brings you confidence in your life?

2. If your confidence were shaken, how do you think would you react?

3. What would it look like if you replaced your confidence in your friend group, your sport or art, your academics, or anything else you excel in with God?

4. Realistically, how confident do you think you are in God?

∼ My Prayer and Reflection ∼

_____

_____

_____

_____

_____

_____

_____

_____

_____

_____

_____

_____

_____

_____

_____

_____

_____

Don't Be Foolish

*Fools make fun of guilt, but the godly
acknowledge it and seek reconciliation.*
PROVERBS 14:9

Making fun of guilt is an easy way to ease your conscience. We might say, "That rule is dumb, I'm not going to follow it" or, "My parents are being ridiculous! They act like I'm a child, but I'm doing what I want anyway." Those type of reactions might make us seem independent or like we're free thinkers, but they are actually foolish reactions.

Solomon was known as the wisest man on the earth, and he wrote the book of Proverbs in the Bible. He was the son of King David, and people came from all over the world to seek Solomon's wisdom. We would be wise to listen to him as well. Solomon said that people who follow God acknowledge their guilt and seek reconciliation. When your conscience lets you know you that you have messed up in some way—whether you've made a mistake morally, shown disrespect toward your parents or teachers, or haven't been loyal and loving to a friend—pay attention! Acknowledge that what you did was wrong; don't brush it off, and don't make fun of it. Own up to it and make it right. You will be wise—and not foolish—when you follow this advice. God will forgive you, and he will help you make things right with others.

Father,

*I admit that I do like to disregard my actions when I know I've messed
up. I make excuses, I blame others, or I will laugh it off. Help me to
change my ways, because I don't want to be foolish. I want to be wise.
I may not like it at the time, but I know it will help me grow and
that is what I want. Thank you for your patience with me. Amen.*

REFLECTION QUESTIONS

1. Do you tend to blame others when you mess up, laugh off your mistakes, or take responsibility for your actions?

2. Why do you think it is so hard to "own" our mistakes?

3. What would it look like for you to follow Solomon's advice, acknowledge your mistakes, and seek reconciliation? Is that hard for you to do? Why or why not?

My Prayer and Reflection

_____

_____

_____

_____

_____

_____

_____

_____

_____

_____

_____

_____

_____

_____

_____

_____

_____

_____

Honor Others

Don't just pretend to love others. Really love them. Hate what is wrong. Hold tightly to what is good. Love each other with genuine affection, and take delight in honoring each other.
ROMANS 12:9-10

To honor someone is to have high respect or great esteem for them. Think about how you treat others in your school. Do you think people can feel your genuine affection for them? Jesus loved everyone at all times. His love never wavered—it didn't matter what popularity or status others had; Jesus had genuine affection for everyone.

Paul writes in Romans, "hate what is wrong." What does that mean to you? What things are "wrong," and what does it mean to hate them? Think about the injustices that you see daily in your world, and hate those and learn to stand for what is right. Don't hate the person, just hate what is wrong and pray for the person who is committing the wrong.

As you walk the halls of your school, play sports, sit in class, or take part in the other activities you do, think about if the people around you can sense that you are honoring them. You may think to yourself, "I'm not Jesus, that is impossible." You are not Jesus, but Jesus is in you and his love can and will shine through you, if you will allow it to happen. God will always show you how to love and honor others.

Father,
Help me to always be honoring to my peers and friends, even to strangers. I want to be known as a loving person to everyone because that is the way you love me. Show me your ways, so when people look at me, they see you. Amen.

REFLECTION QUESTIONS

1. What are some ways you can honor others this week?

2. What does it mean to you to "hate what is wrong and hold tightly to what is good"?

3. What are some things you see that are wrong in the world? What are some things that are good in the world? How can you help create more good in your world?

My Prayer and Reflection

_____

_____

_____

_____

_____

_____

_____

_____

_____

_____

_____

_____

_____

_____

_____

_____

Honor Your Leaders

Dear brothers and sisters, honor those who are your leaders in the Lord's work. They work hard among you and give you spiritual guidance. Show them great respect and wholehearted love because of their work. And live peacefully with each other.

1 THESSALONIANS 5:12–13

It's easy to sit and enjoy events and activities that are put on for us—like youth group retreats or small groups or campus ministry gatherings—but we never think about all the work that goes into them and the spiritual warfare blasting the people who lead those events and activities. A great way to honor your leaders is by praying for them. Prayer is a mighty weapon against the enemy. Pray protection over your leaders and their families. Pray that they will constantly seek God in all they do and that they will be able to discern God's voice.

You can also volunteer to help your leaders. Do they need you to bake brownies for a gathering? Can you bring them their favorite coffee drink to thank them for their hard work? What else can do you do show them that you appreciate the work they do? Another thing you can specifically do for your leaders is to respect them and thank them for their hard work. It is always nice to hear the words "thank you" for the work you do. God has put leaders in your life, and it's your job to honor God by honoring them.

Father,

Thank you for the leaders in my life and all that they do to pour into me and my friends. God, I know they sacrifice a lot in their lives to minister to others. Bless them in a mighty way, and protect them and their families. God, I pray they will continue to walk closely to you, always being aware of your voice and presence. I also pray, Lord, that they will feel the support of others praying for them. Amen.

REFLECTION QUESTIONS

1. Who are your leaders at church, in school, and at your extracurricular activities? Write down their names, then think of ways you can honor them.

2. How can you pray for your leaders this week? What do they need you to pray about?

3. What are some specific ways you can encourage your leaders this week?

My Prayer and Reflection

_____

_____

_____

_____

_____

_____

_____

_____

_____

_____

_____

_____

_____

_____

_____

_____

_____

_____

Hope in Christ

So we don't look at the troubles we can see now; rather, we fix our gaze on things that cannot be seen. For the things we see now will soon be gone, but the things we cannot see will last forever.

2 CORINTHIANS 4:18

The troubles that surround us in our teenage years can feel insurmountable. It is hard not to think that your world is falling apart when you've failed a major exam, a boy has broken your heart, or your friends have turned against you for no apparent reason. Sometimes all of these things happen in the same week—or even in the same day. No matter when they happen, they always feel devastating and impossible to deal with.

During these hard times, it may help you to remember that the things of this earth will fade away, but the things of God will last forever. The failed exam might bring down your grade right now, but in ten years, will it even matter? The breakup may have you reeling in the moment, but God will heal your broken heart and send someone even better for you in his timing. Friends turning against you might make it seem like you'll never have any friends again, but God will get you through this period of rejection and bring stronger friendships into your life.

Keep your eyes open to noticing different ways God meets you in your pain. It could be through wise advice from an adult, worship music that ministers to your heart, or a moment at camp that meets you right where you are. Be on the lookout for his comfort and his hope, because you are a child of the most high God, and he promises to take care of you.

Father,

I can get carried away with my own life, thinking that my own world is everything. Open up my eyes, Lord, to your ways and your perspective. Open up my heart, Lord, to what you want to teach me and show me through my trials. Help me move past my pain and place my hope in you. Amen.

REFLECTION QUESTIONS

1. Why do you think it is so hard to understand that the problems we're having today won't affect us for the rest of our lives?

2. How do you think keeping a perspective of heaven in your daily life would change how you live your life today?

3. What gives you hope when your life seems to be falling apart? How can you do a better job of turning to God for hope?

My Prayer and Reflection

The Peace of God

The Lord is my shepherd; I have all that I need. He lets me rest in green meadows; he leads me beside peaceful streams. He renews my strength. He guides me along right paths, bringing honor to his name.
PSALM 23:1-3

Do you know much about sheep? Sheep are very fearful and skittish animals that need a shepherd in their lives to give them constant care and protection. The Bible tells us that Jesus is our shepherd—"the Lord is my shepherd"—and that God is with us always! He gives us constant care and provision. As our shepherd, God gives us all that we need. He knows that you are a busy teen with a busy schedule who needs rest and relaxation from your demanding, busy life. And so God promises to provide rest for you. God knows that school, friendships, responsibilities, and just your everyday emotions can drain you, and he gives you the strength to tackle another day. On days when you feel like we can't go on, when you can't handle any more friend drama or academic stress, he gives you his peace.

There is peace when we are being led by someone who knows the way. When your life is full of the unknowns about what the future will bring or which direction you're supposed to go, isn't it nice to follow someone who knows you and understands you? As you go through life, always remember that you have your own personal shepherd looking out for you at all times. Your shepherd will guide you, protect you, give you rest and strength, and most important, lead you on the right path as he gives you his peace.

Father,
As I daily trust you to guide my steps and keep me from harm, I pray you will bless me in a mighty way. I want to experience the full measure of your peace. I want to rest in you no matter what is going on in my life. Teach me how to have such peace. Amen.

REFLECTION QUESTIONS

1. When was a time when you felt complete peace? What was happening in your life, and why do you think you felt things were so peaceful?

2. What keeps you from fully trusting God and his ways?

3. What do you think true rest and peace would look like in your life?

My Prayer and Reflection

Forgive Yourself

Jesus replied, "I tell you the truth, Peter—this very night, before the rooster crows, you will deny three times that you even know me." "No!" Peter insisted. "Even if I have to die with you, I will never deny you!"

MATTHEW 26:34-35

Have you ever done something that you feel like you can't forgive yourself for? Often, this involves letting down another person—someone who thought you were their friend. This is what happened with Peter in the Bible. He promised Jesus that he would never deny him, that he would stand beside him until death, and then he did exactly what Jesus said he would do and denied Jesus three times. While Jesus was on trial with the High Priest, Peter stood outside the building where Jesus was being questioned, and three different people asked him if he was a disciple of Jesus. All three times Peter answered no. He let down his friend Jesus three different times, and he must have had trouble forgiving himself for this.

The beauty of Jesus and his love is that he forgives us all, no matter what we have done. Jesus forgives us even when we betray him, when we betray others, when we sin against others or ourselves. Jesus not only forgave Peter, he also built his early church with Peter as the main leader. And Peter must have forgiven himself in order to get past his own guilt and be used by God to set up the church and lead the early leaders.

When you mess up in life—and you will, because we all do—it is important that you learn to accept Jesus' forgiveness and forgive yourself in return. Don't allow shame or guilt to keep you from doing God's work in the future. Learn from your mistakes and move forward.

Father,

Thank you for your love for me. Thank you for always forgiving me for all of my sins, great and small. I pray that as I grow and mature, I will learn from you and always choose to forgive others as you have forgiven me. Sometimes the hardest person to forgive is myself. Show me how to move beyond my past and live a victorious life in you. Amen.

REFLECTION QUESTIONS

1. Which is harder for you—accepting Jesus' forgiveness or forgiving yourself? Why?

2. If you do choose to forgive yourself, how do you think that will open up your life to being able to minister to others?

3. How do you think forgiveness sets you free?

My Prayer and Reflection

_____

_____

_____

_____

_____

_____

_____

_____

_____

_____

_____

_____

_____

_____

_____

_____

God Always Forgives

*O Lord, you are so good, so ready to forgive, so full
of unfailing love for all who ask for your help.*

PSALM 86:5

Think of the most loving person in your life right now. The person who always believes in you, always thinks the best of you, the person who is your biggest cheerleader, the person who no matter what you do or say or how you act will always forgive you and love you. Now take that amazing person and multiply them by a hundred, and you'll be just scratching the surface of how much God loves you. God is not out to get you or punish you, and you are not a disappointment to him. He is always proud of you, he always loves you, he always welcomes you to him, and he always forgives you.

God is such a gracious and forgiving God. Sometimes we believe the lie that God is in heaven looking around to see who is messing up in this life, and when he finds someone who has sinned, he sets out to get them. But the opposite is true. God always forgives, and he always loves. Once you start truly seeing how God views you, it will change the way you live your life. Knowing you have a heavenly Father who adores you will give you an extra measure of confidence. Realizing that God is always on your side will help you not to feel so alone in this world. You will be able to embrace God's great love and all the benefits that come with being his child.

Father,

*Your love doesn't make sense to me, but I am so grateful for it.
I do not feel I deserve so much love or forgiveness, but I gladly
accept it. When I start to doubt, remind me of this verse in
Psalm 86. Keep reminding me until I finally believe it with all
my heart and I know I am loved every day of my life. Amen.*

REFLECTION QUESTIONS

1. Who is your biggest cheerleader in your life? What do they do for you?

2. What do you think about the idea that God is your biggest cheerleader? What could that mean for your life?

3. Why is it sometimes hard to accept God's big love for you?

∽ My Prayer and Reflection ∽

_____

_____

_____

_____

_____

_____

_____

_____

_____

_____

_____

_____

_____

_____

_____

_____

_____

_____

_____

_____

Forgive Others

Make allowance for each other's faults,
and forgive anyone who offends you. Remember,
the Lord forgave you, so you must forgive others.
COLOSSIANS 3:13

Forgiveness is a choice. It is not always an easy choice, and sometimes it is the most difficult thing you can do. Some offenses can be easier to forgive than others. When someone rubs you the wrong way or just kind of annoys you, you can easily forgive them and move on. But when someone deliberately sets out to hurt or betray you, that can be an almost impossible offense to forgive. However, keep in mind that as Christians we are called to forgive. And we can choose to forgive because Christ forgave us.

Another thing to keep in mind is that when you forgive someone, you are releasing that person from having power over you. If you hold a grudge against someone, it is like you are chaining that person to yourself and everywhere you go, they go. Whenever their name is brought up and you remember the offense, the chains grow tighter. Release yourself from these chains, forgive that person, and be set free. Do it for yourself, if for no other reason. You don't forgive because they deserve it—you forgive because you were forgiven first. Be free and forgive.

Father,
Please remind me always that forgiveness is a choice. I can get
stuck in my feelings or in the fact that the other person doesn't
deserve my forgiveness. I also struggle with the idea that if I forgive
someone who doesn't deserve my forgiveness, they "got away" with
hurting me. God, help me to push past these emotions and trust you,
and trust what you say about forgiveness. I want to forgive and
be free from anger and bitterness. Show me the way! Amen.

REFLECTION QUESTIONS

1. What type of offenses are hard for you to forgive? Why do you think it's so hard for you to forgive these things?

2. What would your life look like if you chose to forgive someone? To forgive yourself?

3. What do you think would happen if the person you needed to forgive no longer had power over you? How would that make you feel?

My Prayer and Reflection

_____

_____

_____

_____

_____

_____

_____

_____

_____

_____

_____

_____

_____

_____

_____

_____

_____

_____

Love Others

Love is patient and kind. Love is not jealous or boastful or proud or rude. It does not demand its own way. It is not irritable, and it keeps no record of being wronged. It does not rejoice about injustice but rejoices whenever the truth wins out. Love never gives up, never loses faith, is always hopeful, and endures through every circumstance.

1 CORINTHIANS 13:4–7

"Love well" is a popular saying that appears on random items like coffee mugs and T-shirts. It is easy to say these types of expressions—"love well," "love everyone," or "the world needs love"—but what does it truly mean to love others? The Bible spells it out for us in 1 Corinthians, and once you hear what is involved in loving others, you will realize that loving others is really, really difficult. In fact, some say it is impossible to truly love others without Jesus loving others through you. In our humanness, we can only love to a certain point. We naturally put conditions on our love, and it's easy for us to allow our emotions and feelings to get the best of us.

The Bible tells us that love is patient and kind. Think about the last time you lost patience with your parents, your siblings, or your friends. Love is not jealous, boastful, proud, or rude, but just the opposite. Love celebrates when others achieve or excel, love is humble, and love is always kind to everyone. Love does not demand its own way, but puts others first. Love is not irritable and keeps no records of wrongs, which means love is never in a bad mood and doesn't hold grudges. Love doesn't keep score. Love is the happiest when truth wins out and is the saddest when injustice occurs. Love perseveres and never loses faith in someone, but believes the best and is loyal through all circumstances—good or bad. If you ever wonder how God loves, reread 1 Corinthians 13, which shows better than anything else the true picture of love—the perfect love that is God's love.

Father,

Thank you for loving me. I do not deserve such love, but I am grateful for it. My prayer is that I will slowly learn how to love others this way. I pray, Lord, that you will gently show me an area in which I am lacking your type of love and that I will dedicate myself to work on that. For instance, if I am jealous, show me so that I may confess it and instead learn to celebrate others. Amen.

REFLECTION QUESTIONS

1. When you read about love in 1 Corinthians, do you think it's even possible to love that way?

2. If you could love that way, what would it look like? Give specific examples.
   Love is patient and kind:
   Love is not jealous, boastful, proud, or rude:
   Love does not demand its own way:
   Love is not irritable and keeps no record of wrong:
   Love rejoices in truth:
   Love endures all circumstances:

3. Why do you need Jesus walking with you in your life to experience this kind of love? How do you think he can show you how to love this way?

❧ My Prayer and Reflection ❧

_____

_____

_____

_____

_____

_____

_____

_____

_____

_____

_____

_____

_____

_____

Don't Get Discouraged

Why am I so discouraged? Why is my heart so sad? I will put my hope in God! I will praise him again—my Savior and my God!
PSALM 42:5

Do you ever find yourself becoming discouraged? People tell you that these are the best years of your life, but sometimes it's really hard to see them that way. Sometimes they feel like the worst years of your life, with pressures building up all around you—hard exams, high expectations that teachers, parents, and coaches place on you, and let's not forget relationships and all the drama that can go along with them. At times we can feel like a pressure cooker that is ready to explode. How can we help but become discouraged when so much is happening to us and around us?

David, a man after God's own heart, was also discouraged in life. Not only was David discouraged, he was sad. We all get sad when things look bleak and we don't know how they're going to get better. The death of a friendship or the disappointment of an unmet goal can make us sad, and sadness can come when our home life is not what we want it to be. What are we to do in these times? David tells us to place our hope in God. We are supposed to praise God again and again, even when we are sad. Even in times of despair, lift up your voice and praise God. Praise will make your situation better because it takes your eyes off of your own circumstances and places them on an eternal God who is worthy of our praise. Don't get discouraged—praise God and place your hope in him.

Father,

I know that I will be discouraged and sad in my life, but it brings me comfort to know that I am not alone. The antidote to being discouraged and sad is to praise you, God. Help me to remember that! When I get discouraged, I tend to wallow in self-pity, but instead help me to raise my eyes to you. Amen.

REFLECTION QUESTIONS

1. Are you in a season of sadness in your life right now? What is happening, and how are you dealing with the sadness?

2. What do you think "placing your hope in God" looks like?

3. What is holding you back from placing your hope in God fully?

My Prayer and Reflection

_____

_____

_____

_____

_____

_____

_____

_____

_____

_____

_____

_____

_____

_____

_____

_____

_____

_____

Pray Nonstop

Never stop praying.
1 THESSALONIANS 5:17

Can you have a best friend without talking to your best friend? Can you have any type of meaningful relationship with someone without talking with them? The answer is no. We grow close to someone when we share our thoughts, our feelings, our highs and lows with them. We grow close when we bare our souls to someone and share our most secret and intimate thoughts with them. Did you know that prayer is just talking to God? Prayer builds your relationship with God because you are sharing your heart with him, just like you would with a best friend.

When your life is super busy and full, prayer can be an afterthought. But the Bible tells us to never stop praying. Praying should be as easy as breathing for us. When you are waking up in the morning, lift up a prayer of thankfulness to God for another day. As you get ready for school, involve God in your day, telling him what all you have going on and raising any requests or burdens that are on your heart. When you get to school and you're walking through the halls, possibly passing by people who you don't care for, lift those thoughts up to him as you're walking. Ask God to show you how to love those who hurt you. Before you eat your meals, say a prayer of thankfulness (you can even do this with your eyes open). As you take tests, step onto the sports field, enter your drama or art class, or get out your band instrument, be in constant prayer that God will be glorified in all that you do. As you go home from school, thank God for another day of life on this earth. Thank him for the many blessings you experienced or the hard day that you went through. When you walk into your home, give your mom and dad a hug and thank God for them. As you lay your head down to go to sleep, after doing your homework or texting with friends, tell God about your day, your highs and lows, and all your feelings.

Praying nonstop isn't just something to add to your to-do list. It's a way to draw you closer to your heavenly Father, who thinks you are amazing and wants a relationship with you.

Father,
Thank you for always listening to me. I want a deeper relationship
with you, and if that comes by talking to you nonstop,
I'll try it. Gently remind me to look to you, and be
brave enough to open my heart and soul to you. Amen.

REFLECTION QUESTIONS

1. What are some things that keep you from praying?

2. What does "praying nonstop" mean to you? Do you think it is possible to do this? Why or why not?

3. What steps can you take this week to get one step closer to praying nonstop?

‿ My Prayer and Reflection ‿

God's Big Love

*For this is how God loved the world: He gave
his one and only Son, so that everyone who
believes in him will not perish but have eternal life.*

JOHN 3:16

John 3:16 is such a simple verse, but it has had such a huge impact on all of humankind. God loved the world and from that love he wanted a relationship with people. But because humans were full of sin, a sacrifice had to be paid for our sin, because God is a holy God. The sacrifice needed to be pure and holy, and the only person who could be that sacrifice was Jesus. Therefore, God in his great love for us sent his one and only Son as a payment for our sin. Not only did God send his Son, Jesus, but Jesus went willingly. Salvation is easy! If you believe in Jesus, you will not perish or die, but you will live forever with God and Jesus in heaven. See what I mean by a simple verse with a huge impact?

No one can earn this gift, pay for this gift, or work their way toward this gift. It is a gift sent from God directly to you and me and the entire world. This type of love is hard for us humans to comprehend, because whether we want to admit it or not, our love usually has strings attached. It is easy for us to believe that God has strings attached to his love too, but he doesn't. God is pure in his motives of loving us and wanting a relationship with us. His love is big!

Father,

*Thank you for your big love. That sentence is becoming
a theme in my prayer life, because every day you remind
me how much you love me, and I cannot thank you enough.
Thank you for loving me, even in my sin. Thank you for your Son,
Jesus, and how he gave up his life for humankind. God, teach me
how to love like you love. Help me to love others unconditionally
in the way that you love me and the rest of the world. Amen.*

REFLECTION QUESTIONS

1. Is John 3:16 easy for you to accept, or is it difficult to understand? Why?
2. What does this verse mean to you in your life?
3. How can you start loving others the way God loves you?

~ My Prayer and Reflection ~

_____

_____

_____

_____

_____

_____

_____

_____

_____

_____

_____

_____

_____

_____

_____

_____

_____

_____

_____

_____

_____

Forever God

*Before the mountains were born, before you gave birth to
the earth and the world, from beginning to end, you are God.*

PSALM 90:2

Sometimes it can be hard to know who to trust. A friend promises that she'll keep something confidential that you told her as a secret, but then the temptation is too great and she tells your secret to others. You like a guy and think you can trust him, but then you find out that he's been texting other girls. You're promised a spot on the team or a role in the play, but then you find out you didn't make it. Trusting can be hard.

There is someone you can always trust, and that someone is God. We serve a God who has been in existence from the beginning of time. Think about that for a moment. Can you even comprehend it? It is hard for our minds to think in an infinite way. But the fact that God has been around since before the earth was created is incredible. This one fact should give us confidence that he is a God worth following and, more importantly, someone in whom we can place our trust. Who better to trust than a God that has created everything and everyone in the world? A God who loves and adores us so much that he gave his only Son for us to have a relationship with him? A God who has a love so big, it lasts an eternity?

God has written you into his story that has been in the works since the beginning of time. How amazing is that? As you go about your life this week, try to remind yourself that the God you trust has a love that lasts for all of eternity, and that love is also for you. Nothing is too big for him, no mountain too high, no valley too low. He is our forever God, and we can always trust him.

Father,

*What an amazing thought that you are eternal. You have
no beginning and no end. I love that I can place my trust in
you and that you are trustworthy. Thank you for hearing
my prayers and seeing me in all of your creation. God,
I place my life in your hands, and I love and trust you. Amen.*

REFLECTION QUESTIONS

1. What do you think it would be like to have no beginning and no end?

2. Think about the history of this world and the fact that God was there for every moment of it. Does that give you the confidence that God can handle your troubles? Why or why not?

3. What would it look like if you trusted an infinite God with all your cares? How would that affect your life?

⤳ My Prayer and Reflection ⤳

_____

_____

_____

_____

_____

_____

_____

_____

_____

_____

_____

_____

_____

_____

_____

_____

God Is Good

Taste and see that the Lord is good.
Oh, the joys of those who take refuge in him!
PSALM 34:8

When you taste something, you probably have an automatic response: good or bad. Maybe sushi, cookie dough ice cream, and mangoes are in your "good" category. And you'd rate overcooked scrambled eggs, pumpkin pie, and bananas as "bad." But we don't all have the same tastes in food. Your best friend's "good" and "bad" could be wildly different from your own.

This Bible passage might sound kind of odd: "Taste and see that the Lord is good." What does this even mean? Well, have you ever just sat and contemplated the goodness of God? The God who made the universe is a good and loving God. Even when bad things are happening all around us, the Bible tells us that he will work all things together for good, for those who love the Lord (Romans 8:28). We can stand on that promise because not only is God good, he is also faithful and trustworthy. Sometimes in life, we must stand on these truths and keep reminding ourselves over and over that the Lord is good.

Think of all the good that God has created in this world—the birth of a baby, magnificent scenes of nature all over the globe, the galaxies in the sky, the beauty of an eagle soaring above. The list could go on forever. What joy we have when we trust fully in him. What joy we experience in life when we accept God as our refuge, our safe place. When our world is falling apart, we will not live in fear if we run to him, because he will protect us, lead us, and love us. When we start to follow Christ, we will experience his goodness.

Father,

Thank you for your goodness. Thank you for showing me your goodness and beauty in the natural world, in the kindness of other people, and in yourself. God, I pray that I will learn to trust you with all my heart and run to you for protection when I am in distress or in need. Thank you for being trustworthy. When my world does not look "good," gently remind me that you are good, all the time. Amen.

REFLECTION QUESTIONS

1. What are some ways you see—or "taste"—that God is good?

2. Can you think of a time in your life where you saw God work "all things together for good"? What happened during this time?

3. What would it look like for you for God to be your refuge and your safe place?

My Prayer and Reflection

_____

_____

_____

_____

_____

_____

_____

_____

_____

_____

_____

_____

_____

_____

_____

_____

_____

God Has a Plan for Your Life

This is what the Scriptures mean when they say,
"No eye has seen, no ear has heard, and no mind has
imagined what God has prepared for those who love him."
1 CORINTHIANS 2:9

Your teenage years can be exciting—new opportunities, new beginnings, and new worlds opening up for you. These years can also be a little scary, especially when it feels like everyone else knows exactly what they want to do with their life and you don't have a clue what to do with yours. When you feel lost and alone during these times, remember that you are not alone and that God does have a plan for your life. He promises to guide and direct you in your life if you lean into him (Proverbs 3:5-6).

You can rest in the fact that God is sovereign and that he wants good for you. It is sort of like getting on an airplane and taking a trip to the other side of the world. You may not know how to fly the plane, but the pilot does. The pilot is trained and skilled to tackle anything and everything that will come their way on that flight. You as the passenger only need to sit back, relax, and place your faith in the pilot. It is the same with God. God is the pilot in your life. He knows the way, so all you have to do is walk with him. Stay in step with him on a daily basis, and he will guide your steps all the way. How do you stay in step with God? Study his word and learn about his character, his majesty, and his love for you. Develop a prayer life, which is basically an ongoing conversation with God. Tell him your fears, your dreams, your hurts, and your secrets that you are too afraid to share with anyone else. Listen to God and look for his voice in your life. Remember that he has a plan, and he's excited to share that plan with you.

Father,
You have a plan for my life, and for that I am grateful.
Sometimes I think I know what is best for my life,
but help me to trust in you for the final decision. Show me
how to walk with you. Teach me how to listen to your voice when
you are talking with me. I want to know and trust you more. Amen.

REFLECTION QUESTIONS

1. Do you have a plan for your life, or do you feel like you don't have a clue as to what your future will look like?

2. How does it make you feel to know that God has a plan for your life?

3. What steps can you take this week to trust God with the plans he has for your life?

My Prayer and Reflection

_____

_____

_____

_____

_____

_____

_____

_____

_____

_____

_____

_____

_____

_____

_____

_____

_____

God Gives Us Confidence

I pray that God, the source of hope, will fill you completely with joy and peace because you trust in him. Then you will overflow with confident hope through the power of the Holy Spirit.

ROMANS 15:13

Who doesn't want to be confident in life? Everyone looks up to confident people. In your teen years, it can be easy to lose the self-confidence you so naturally possessed as a little kid. But confidence—*real* confidence—is yours for the taking. In God's world, confidence comes when we place our trust not in ourselves but in God. When we decide to put him first above our own interests and desires, he will give us the confidence we need. God is the source of our hope, not us. God is the source of our joy and peace. God is the source of our confidence. This way of thinking is so counterintuitive. The world gives us the exact opposite message. The world says that we need to be confident in our own abilities, talents, and gifts. The world says that to attain joy, we need to be doing things in our lives that bring us joy, that we need to do what makes us happy, whether those things are good or not.

It is great to put your confidence in yourself, until you fail. When you fail, and we all do at some point in our lives, we feel like because we messed up, *we* are a failure. Sometimes we can get so down on ourselves that it is hard to pull ourselves back up. And that makes us afraid to try again, because what if we "fail" again? When we put our trust in God, we can't fail. That's because he will never fail us. God cannot fail—it is impossible. God gives you a choice. Will you place your trust in yourself and in your own merit, or will you place it in an almighty God who will in return give you confidence, joy, and peace? Real confidence comes from trusting in a confident God.

Father,
I want to place all my trust in you. Help me keep my eyes focused on what your word says and not pay attention to what the world says. I want my confidence to be in you, and I want your joy and peace in my life. Show me the way. Amen.

REFLECTION QUESTIONS

1. Who is the most confident person you know? What do you admire about their confidence?

2. Where do the most confident people put their trust? How is this apparent in their lives?

3. What would it look like for you to fully place your trust in God? How do you think your life—and your confidence—would look different than it does now?

My Prayer and Reflection

_____

_____

_____

_____

_____

_____

_____

_____

_____

_____

_____

_____

_____

_____

_____

_____

_____

Desire for God

As the deer longs for streams of water,
so I long for you, O God. I thirst for God, the living God.
PSALM 42:1-2

Have you ever thought about this idea of "longing" for God? It is easy to long for God when we are in trouble. In fact, the first thing we normally do when things start going wrong in our lives is to cry out for God to help us. Right? But do we also long for God when things are going well? When our friends are being nice, when our grades are good, when our relationship with our parents is strong, when we have plenty of money to do what we want to do and get what we want to get, when we're having a lot of success in life, when we're feeling happy and not stressed out—do we long for God then? Or is he just an afterthought?

Take a look at Psalm 42:1-2 again. What it is saying to us? The first thing we notice is that a deer longs for streams of water. That's because deer must have water. They cannot survive without water. Therefore, they love to be near water, where they know they can easily have a source to quench their thirst. Do we thirst for God? Do we thirst for his knowledge, his direction, his love, and his wisdom? I know that in my life, the times when I have thirsted for God, I had to make him a priority, whether things were going good or bad. It took discipline. Discipline to set my clock and have my time with God at a certain time every day. Then, after I'd made a habit of spending time with God, I would miss it if I skipped it for some reason. It is doable to long and thirst for God, to have a desire to spend time with him, but we must first start by being intentional about spending time with him. Long for God when you're having a bad day, but start making a habit of longing for him in the good days too.

Father,

This illustration of a deer longing for streams of water is such a beautiful
picture of the way my life could look with you. I truly want to depend
on you for my every need, want, and desire. I truly want to be that close
to you. I want to be intentional, and I am going to make a point to
do just that—being intentional with my time with you, God. Amen.

REFLECTION QUESTIONS

1. What can you do to be more intentional in your walk with the Lord?

2. Do you find it's easier to long for God when times are good, or when times are bad? Why do you think this is the case?

3. What do you think your life would look like if you focused on spending time with God every day, no matter what was happening?

❧ My Prayer and Reflection ❧

_____

_____

_____

_____

_____

_____

_____

_____

_____

_____

_____

_____

_____

_____

_____

_____

Be Still and Know God

*Be still, and know that I am God! I will be honored by
every nation. I will be honored throughout the world.*
PSALM 46:10

How do you get to know a person? You might think you "know" someone if you follow them on social media and see what they post every day. But do you really know that person? When you see them in person (*if* you see them in person), do you feel like you're actually friends?

We might say that we "know" God, but how well do we really know him? Do we really understand him? Does God seem like some mysterious, invisible being, or does he seem real to us? How do we get to know him? Is that even possible? In the Bible, David was known to be a man after God's own heart, someone who knew God in an intimate way. And that's why he wrote in Psalm 46:10, "Be still, and know that I am God!" He understood that we can only know God if we spend time with him—and that part of that time spent with him is just hanging out in silence, enjoying his company and resting in his presence.

To "be still" is one of the hardest things to do—especially if it involves putting down our phones, quieting our minds, forgetting everything we're stressed and worried about, and just focusing on God. A lot of the time, spending time in God's creation can help us to be still. Nature is a great place to sit and be still and find God. You can see God in nature all around you. When we sit and truly think about all that God created and how he created all things, when we observe his workmanship in action, we at least begin to understand how majestic he is. Jesus said, "even the rocks will cry out" (Luke 19:40) to sing his praises. Find a special place to go where you can "be still" and start getting to truly *know* the God who created you and loves you.

Father,

*Help me learn to be still. Show me how to sit quietly before you and
learn how to "know" you more. I want to know you on a deeper level.
I want you to walk beside me, I want to be able to hear your voice.
You are the same God, yesterday, today, and tomorrow. If David knew
you, then I can know you too. Thank you for knowing me. Amen.*

REFLECTION QUESTIONS

1. What do you think it means to really "know" someone?

2. What do you think it means to "be still" before God? What would "being still" mean for you? What are some ways you can go about doing this? (Hint: think of what you might need to stop doing too.)

3. Where do you feel closest to God? What do you feel when you go to that place?

My Prayer and Reflection

_____

_____

_____

_____

_____

_____

_____

_____

_____

_____

_____

_____

_____

_____

_____

_____

_____

Don't Have a Critical Spirit

Do not judge others, and you will not be judged.
For you will be treated as you treat others.
MATTHEW 7:1-2

It is so easy to look around and be critical of others, especially people who are not like us. We may look at other people and think to ourselves, "They are so weird, so strange, so different." Or we may think, "They think they're better than me—I bet they're such a snob." Whatever the reason is for judging others, judging never a good thing to do. Jesus is very clear in Matthew when he says, "Do not judge." It can't get any more direct than that. He drives his point home by telling us that we will be treated the same way we treat others. That statement alone should get our attention and make us think about how we treat other people.

You might be thinking, "What does it really matter if I am just being critical in my mind?" However, the more you think something, the more it gets into your heart, and then the next thing you know, you will start acting on that thought. You might start saying out loud the things that you are thinking, and next thing you know, you've hurt someone's feelings or you've developed a reputation as a gossip. So, train your mind not to be critical of others but instead to love people and accept them the way they are.

Check in with yourself on a regular basis: Am I treating others well? Am I criticizing or judging others? These are sobering questions to ask, but the more self-aware we are, the less likely we will be to have a critical spirit and the more we will treat others the way Jesus treats them.

Father,

I admit I can be critical of others. Maybe I am critical because deep down I am insecure, or maybe I just don't like it when people are different than me. Whatever the reason, I don't want to be that way. Give me love for others, the way you love them. Help me to accept and treat others in the best way possible. Amen.

REFLECTION QUESTIONS

1. Do you find yourself being critical of other people? In what ways?

2. This week, notice how you "treat" other people. Do your actions show love or just mere tolerance of others?

3. In what ways can you treat others better this week? Make a list of the people you are going to reach out to with kindness.

My Prayer and Reflection

Your Words Matter

*And I tell you this, you must give an account on
judgement day for every idle word you speak.*
MATTHEW 12:36

As Christians, our sins have already been judged. They were paid for on the cross when Jesus died. We will, however, still need to give an account for the sins Jesus died for, including our words. Words that we throw out at times without much thought behind them. Words that can hurt another person deeply, even to the point where friendships and ruined. Words that can make a person feel either loved and accepted, or disliked and excluded. Bottom line: your words matter. There is an old saying, "Think before you speak," which is good advice for all of us.

Think about it—even something as small and fleeting as our words will have to be accounted for before God. So start now, while you are still defining who you are, to be mindful of your words. When you realize your words have been hurtful or have damaged another person, confess that before God and then go and ask forgiveness from the person you offended. If your words are any form of profanity, confess that to God as well. Keep short accounts with your words. Move on from the times you used hurtful words, and practice using words that show love and encouragement. The more you become self-aware of the things you say, the better you will be. The words you speak matter.

Father,

*Help me to be aware of all of my words. I want my words to build others
up and not tear them down. I want my words to glorify you and not be
offensive to others. Now that I understand how much my words truly
matter, help me to practice self-discipline in this area of my life. Amen.*

REFLECTION QUESTIONS

1. What do you think it means to be accountable for the words you say?

2. What words have you spoken recently that have showed love and acceptance to others? What words have you spoken that have showed unkindness and exclusion? Which type of words come most naturally for you?

3. Why do you think it's important to confess your words before God when your words are not good?

ℰ My Prayer and Reflection ℰ

_____

_____

_____

_____

_____

_____

_____

_____

_____

_____

_____

_____

_____

_____

_____

_____

_____

_____

_____

Esther's Story

Mordecai sent this reply to Esther: "Don't think for a moment that because you're in the palace you will escape when all other Jews are killed. If you keep quiet at a time like this, deliverance and relief for the Jews will arise from some other place, but you and your relatives will die. Who knows if perhaps you were made queen for just such a time as this?"

ESTHER 4:13-14

The story of Esther is like a modern-day Cinderella story. Esther is chosen to be queen of a great empire. She goes from rags to riches overnight. When she is chosen to be queen, the king does not know she is of Jewish decent because Esther kept that a secret. The story progresses when a man in the kingdom, Haman, becomes angry at the Jews and plots to have them all killed. The king agrees to Haman's plan, and the date is set for the annihilation of the Jewish nation. So far, this sounds like a Disney movie, only way more intense!

In the next scene, Mordecai, Esther's uncle, asks Esther to go before the king and plead the case of the Jews and save her people. Esther is afraid to do this, because if she goes into the king's presence without being summoned, he could kill her on the spot. Verse 13 of today's passage shows Mordecai's reply to Esther. Mordecai challenges Esther to step out in faith and do what was is right to save a whole nation. Mordecai lets Esther know, "Perhaps this is the whole reason you were chosen as queen!" Sometimes God places each of us in an impossible situation in order to accomplish his work. It can be scary to step out in faith, but you never know what weighs in the balance. But have courage and have faith—be like Esther and follow God.

Father,

Thank you for these Old Testament stories that show how real people were scared to step out in faith, but how when they did, the results were great. Give me the courage, Lord, to be willing to do the hard stuff for your kingdom and your glory. Amen.

REFLECTION QUESTIONS

1. Can you relate to Esther's story? What was a time when you were afraid to do the right thing?

2. How do you feel about Mordecai's response? What would you have thought if you were Esther?

3. Is it hard for you to step out in faith? Why or why not? What do you think would happen if you did choose to step out in faith despite your fears?

My Prayer and Reflection

_____

_____

_____

_____

_____

_____

_____

_____

_____

_____

_____

_____

_____

_____

_____

_____

_____

_____

_____

_____

_____

The Need for Prayer

*Then Esther sent this reply to Mordecai: "Go and gather together
all the Jews of Susa and fast for me. Do not eat or drink for three
days, night or day. My maids and I will do the same. And then, though
it is against the law, I will go in to see the king. If I must die, I must die."*

ESTHER 4:15-16

We're back to Esther's story (because it's just that *good*). In order for Esther to carry out her mission, she knew she could not do it with her own courage and strength. She needed prayer from the entire Jewish nation. This task was too big for her. Esther wasn't just asking for the Jews to pray once—she was asking them to fast and pray for three entire days.

Sometimes God lays something on our hearts, and we know instantly that we cannot do it by ourselves. In these times, don't forget your most valuable asset as a Christian—the power of prayer. You and I have the ability to approach the throne of God itself and ask God for what we want. As you approach God in prayer, keep in mind that he wants to hear your heart, he wants to help you in whatever way he can, and that he is a good God.

The story of Esther is so beautiful. After three days of the Jewish people fasting and praying, Esther bravely went before the king and made her request. God opened up the king's heart, and the king saved the Jewish people. The king had Haman killed in their place. God heard Esther and the Jewish people's prayers, and he saved them. Prayer is so powerful—and so is our wonderful God!

Father,

*Thank you for always listening to my prayers. Thank you
for always being a good God and for giving me the courage
and strength to do the things I think I cannot do. Please help
me to continue to trust in you and to be bold for you. Amen.*

REFLECTION QUESTIONS

1. What part of this story can you relate to?

2. When you are faced with a difficult decision or situation, is it hard for you to pause and pray before you tackle it? Why or why not?

3. Do you think God asks more of us than we can accomplish on our own? Why or why not?

My Prayer and Reflection

_____

_____

_____

_____

_____

_____

_____

_____

_____

_____

_____

_____

_____

_____

_____

_____

_____

_____

Trust

*But those who trust in the L*ORD *will find new strength.*
They will soar high on wings like eagles. They will
run and not grow weary. They will walk and not faint.
ISAIAH 40:31

Giving someone your trust is not always easy. There is so much risk involved in trusting. All the questions arise in your mind: "What if they disappoint me?" "What if they reject me?" "What if they don't keep their promises?" It's not always easy to trust people, but you can always trust God. He will never disappoint you. He will never reject you. He will always keep his promises. He is trustworthy. When you step out in faith and trust God, you always get something good in return, and you will find new strength.

Most of the time when we are reaching out to God for his help, we have already come to the realization that we cannot do something on our own. We need help. Usually in this stage, we are feeling kind of desperate, because we have already tried everything else. God will always give us strength in these times. The strength God gives us is his strength, not ours. So, make it a habit to trust God, even if you have a hard time with trust. God will not disappoint you. He is good, and he wants good things for you because you are his child and he loves you.

Father,
Thank you for loving me. Thank you that I can trust you
and that you are faithful. It is hard to trust sometimes,
but I know in my heart that you are trustworthy.
Give me the faith to trust. I want to rest in you. Amen.

REFLECTION QUESTIONS

1. Why do you sometimes find it hard to trust others?

2. Do you believe that God is worthy of your trust? Why or why not?

3. What do you think your life would look like if you fully trusted God in all aspects of your life?

My Prayer and Reflection

_____

_____

_____

_____

_____

_____

_____

_____

_____

_____

_____

_____

_____

_____

_____

_____

_____

_____

_____

_____

God Is Love

But anyone who does not love does not know God, for God is love.
1 JOHN 4:8

As humans we tend to love on a conditional basis. If someone is nice to us, accepting of us, or generous to us, then we may choose to love them. If someone is hurtful to us, excludes us, or says mean things about us, then we may choose to not love them. We like the people who like us, and we don't like the people who don't like us. God, however, is not like that. God loves all of us, all the time, and his love is unconditional. Love is not just a characteristic of God or something he chooses to do. He IS love—it is who he is.

It is so important that we realize this fact about God because it will completely change the way we view him. So many people have this belief that God is up in heaven just waiting for us to mess up, and when we do he is ready to punish us. Yet God is the opposite. He loves all the time. He is patient and long-suffering with us. If you view God in this way, you will want to draw close to him. You will begin to involve him in every aspect of your life because you know he is for you, not against you. You will trust God, which is crucial in your walk with him. You can't have a full relationship with someone unless you trust them. Always remember that God is love, and he is full of love for you.

Father,
Thank you for your love. I want to always remember this
fact about you, so when I start to doubt you, gently remind me
who you are. You don't love like I love. You don't choose to give your
love to some people and not to others. Your love is unconditional,
and it's for all of us. Thank you so much for loving me. Amen.

REFLECTION QUESTIONS

1. Why is it hard to fully believe that God loves us all the time, even when we mess up?

2. If you started to believe with all your heart that God always loves you, how would that change your view of God? How would it change how you live your life?

3. What does unconditional love mean to you? How good are you at showing unconditional love to others?

❧ My Prayer and Reflection ❧

_____

_____

_____

_____

_____

_____

_____

_____

_____

_____

_____

_____

_____

_____

_____

_____

The Presence of God

*For your presence among us sets your people
and me apart from all other people on the earth.*
EXODUS 33:16

It's trendy today to talk about being "fully present." But what does that really mean? You can say you're "fully present" when you're talking to a friend, but is that actually possible to do? You're listening to your friend and you truly do care about her, but sometimes your mind wanders to your own stuff. You're human, you're not perfect, and you just can't help it. God, however, is fully present in your life—always. He's always there with you, always ready to hear you when you talk to him. He hangs on your every word. God tells us that he will never leave us (John 14:16). His presence is among us, and he is always fully present with us.

You might be wondering, how do I do that? How do I enter into the presence of God? Is that even possible? Yes, it is possible. We must pursue God. When we want something in life, whether it is a relationship, good grades, a job, or a leadership position, we pursue that thing. We learn about it, takes notes on how to achieve our goal, ask the right questions, and spend time with that person or learning about that topic. It is the same with God. If you want to experience God's presence in your life, pursue him with all your heart and soul. Be fully present when you spend time with him. Focus on him, read the Bible, and learn all you can about him. God always welcomes you into his presence.

Father,

*Thank you, Lord, that you will never leave me. That is very
comforting. I am thankful that you are always with me,
guiding me in my life. Teach me how to pursue you. Help me
to enter into your presence and be "all there" when I'm with you.
Sometimes when I read the Bible, it is confusing to me. I am
asking you to open my eyes and heart to your word. Amen.*

REFLECTION QUESTIONS

1. What do you think it means to pursue God? What do you think it means to be in his presence?

2. Does the thought of pursuing God excite you, scare you, or are you indifferent to it? Why?

3. If you did pursue God with all your heart, how do you think your life would change?

My Prayer and Reflection

_____

_____

_____

_____

_____

_____

_____

_____

_____

_____

_____

_____

_____

_____

_____

_____

Walk Humbly

No, O people, the LORD has told you what is good,
and this is what he requires of you: to do what is right,
to love mercy, and to walk humbly with your God.
MICAH 6:8

In the Bible, God tells us that he does not like pride (Proverbs 16:18). If we want to learn how to be in the presence of God, then we must walk humbly before God. Pride does not have a place in God's world. There is nothing to be proud of in the presence of God. Everything we have—whether it's our gorgeous brown eyes, our feet that are perfectly arched for ballet, our quick mind and tongue that make us fearsome at debate, or even our welcoming nature that makes it easy for us to make friends—comes directly from God. He is the creator of all, and it is through God that we accomplish anything in life. Apart from him, we can do nothing. That's why we need to be grateful and humble in his presence.

Once we start practicing this attitude of walking humbly, it will slowly begin to change our relationship with God. And it will begin to change us. God tells us to draw near to him and he will draw near to us. But in order to draw near to him, we need to acknowledge that he is God and we are not. He knows the best path for our life, and we should gladly follow him. That is where humility comes in. It is hard to give up control. It's easy to want to follow our own path and to take credit for our talents and successes. But God wants us to do what is right, and part of doing what is right is walking humbly with God.

Father,

I am thankful that if I draw near to you, you will draw near to me.
What a blessing! Teach me how to be humble before you. I do have
a lot of pride. I like to take credit for my talents and my successes,
but I know that every good thing comes from you. Show me how
to live a humble life and to give all the credit and glory to you. Amen.

REFLECTION QUESTIONS

1. What does "walk humbly before God" mean to you?

2. What are some things in your life that you are proud of? How can you give God the credit for these things?

3. What can you do to draw near to God this week?

My Prayer and Reflection

_____

_____

_____

_____

_____

_____

_____

_____

_____

_____

_____

_____

_____

_____

_____

_____

_____

_____

_____

Heart of the Matter

*And you must love the LORD your God with all
your heart, all your soul, and all your strength.*
DEUTERONOMY 6:5

Where your heart is, your body will follow. Think about it—when you love something, you go after it. The food you love, you eat. The sports you love, you play. The people you love, you have a relationship with them and spend lots of time with them. It is the same principle with God. When we love God, we should be "all in." We should be spending time with him every day, giving our relationship with him our whole heart, our whole soul, and all of our strength. Our hearts should always be tuned in to God.

One way to be "all in" with God is to read his word. If you want to know God, *really* know him, read the Bible. There, you will learn so much about his character, what is important to him, what pleases him, what angers him, and what he wants you to do and how he wants you to live. You will learn how consistent he is and how much he loves you. Bring God into your daily life, not just when things aren't going well. Figure out how you connect best with God, whether it is through nature, music, studying the Bible, or going to church. Anything that makes you want to draw near to him, pursue those things. God is real and he is wanting a relationship with you. Love God with all your heart, all your soul, all your mind, and all your strength. That is the heart of the matter.

Father,
Teach me what it would look like to love you with all my heart,
soul, and strength. Show me how I can be "all in" in our relationship.
I want that, but at times I am at a loss because sometimes you
can feel very distant to me. However, I know you are not far away,
so help me move past my feelings and get to the truth. Amen.

REFLECTION QUESTIONS

1. What do you think it means to love God with all your heart, soul, and strength?

2. What would it look like for you to be "all in" with God?

3. Is there anything in your life that is holding you back from being "all in" with him?

My Prayer and Reflection

Guard Your Heart

Guard your heart above all else,
for it determines the course of your life.
PROVERBS 4:23

What is your most treasured possession? Is it your phone? Do you throw your phone around, or are you careful with it and make sure you don't drop it? Do you have a drop-proof case on it to give it extra protection? Do you make sure it's always charged? Do you regularly update your phone and get new apps for it? If you answered yes, that makes sense, because when something is valuable, you take extra measures to take care of it and to keep it safe and away from harm.

As a teenager, your heart can be vulnerable and easily broken. Just like you protect your phone to ensure it doesn't get broken, you need to do the same thing with your heart. Be mindful of your heart and take extra measures to protect it. One way you can do this is by being careful about the people you spend time with. Watch how your friends respond to situations, and decide early on if they are trustworthy or if they're quick to gossip about others and spread rumors. If they don't seem like they care about others, you may not want to trust them fully with your loyalty. If you find yourself feeling bad about yourself or other people after hanging out with your friends, maybe it's time to find some better friends. God wants you to protect your heart, because your heart will determine the course of your life.

Father,
Give me the gift of discernment and help me not
to rush so quickly into a relationship before I can see
the other person's character. I want to believe everyone,
but I know in my heart that not everyone is worthy
of my trust. Help me to learn who I can trust my heart
with and who I need to keep my guard up with. Amen.

REFLECTION QUESTIONS

1. Are you one to quickly make friendships, or are you more skeptical of people? How do you think this has affected your relationships?

2. Why do you think is it wise to guard your heart?

3. What measures can you set up to better protect your heart?

∾ My Prayer and Reflection ∾

_____

_____

_____

_____

_____

_____

_____

_____

_____

_____

_____

_____

_____

_____

_____

_____

_____

_____

_____

DAY 66 — *Immeasurably More*

Now all glory to God, who is able, through his mighty power at work within us, to accomplish infinitely more than we might ask or think.

EPHESIANS 3:20

How many times a day do you feel clueless? How many times have you thought to yourself, *What do I do in this situation?* How many times have you been asked to do something and you have no idea where to begin? How many times has your mind gone completely blank when you're faced with a tough essay question or a friend who needs you to say just the right thing? It's easy to feel like you don't have a clue when you're in a pressure situation.

There is good news for you! Jesus' power is working within us. Through him we are able to do immeasurably more than we can even imagine. When we feel like we don't have another ounce of energy to continue, Jesus provides that energy for us. When we feel our patience has come to an end with our teachers, our parents, our coaches, or our friends, if we call on Jesus, he will come through for us and give us the patience we need.

When you are weak, he is strong. You can't do this life on your own. You need a Savior. You need the power of Jesus working through you—always. When you rely on him, he will provide everything you need. Today, when you get to the end of your rope and feel like you don't have a clue what to do next, call out to him and ask him to give you immeasurably more.

Father,

Thank you for always being with me. I can't do this life on my own—I need you. Thank you for knowing this before I ever did and for preparing a way for me. Thank you that through your Son, Jesus, I can accomplish more than I ever dreamed of accomplishing. Amen.

REFLECTION QUESTIONS

1. What are some situations when you have felt completely clueless about what to do next? How do you feel when you've reached the end of your rope?

2. Do you feel like you can do immeasurable more with Jesus? Why or why not?

3. What do you think it would look like if Jesus worked through you to allow you to accomplish more in your life?

❧ My Prayer and Reflection ☙

_____

_____

_____

_____

_____

_____

_____

_____

_____

_____

_____

_____

_____

_____

_____

_____

Take a Moment

Let all that I am wait quietly before God, for my hope is in him.
PSALM 62:5

Have you ever had one of those crazy-busy weeks? A week where you're constantly studying, volunteering, running from one activity to the next, trying to stay connected to your friends, and barely eating and sleeping? Between school and social stuff and all your activities, you hardly have time to yourself. But sometimes you need to slow down and just rest in God. When you slow down, you may be tempted to think you are being lazy. But we all need to hit pause from time to time.

What do you think sitting quietly before the Lord looks like? You might want to take a walk to observe something in nature you would normally take for granted and have never taken the time to notice. You could grab coffee or smoothies with a friend and just talk, listening to each other and really hearing what is on the other person's heart. You could go to lunch or bake cookies with your mom, listening to her wisdom and asking about what is going on in her world. You might want to listen to some worship music or play the piano or guitar while you spend time in God's presence. You could even just sit on your couch or your bed and hang out with God, reading your Bible, sharing your heart with him, and just sitting in his presence.

These simple things might feel weird for you if you're used to being super busy. They might almost feel childlike, but hitting the pause button can be life-giving. Try it today. Take a moment, pause, and see what happens. You just might be surprised by the result.

Father,

I want to find rest in you. Teach me how to slow down; it's so hard for me to do. I feel like my life is speeding by, faster and faster each day. But I don't want to look back on these years and realize that I was so busy that I forgot about the most important thing in my life—you. Help me to take a moment and hit pause when I need to. Amen.

REFLECTION QUESTIONS

1. Do you ever take time to rest during the day, or are you always go-go-going?

2. If it's hard for you to rest, why do you think you have trouble with it?

3. What are some ways you can take a moment and rest in God? (hanging out in nature, listening to or playing music, drawing or painting, spending time talking about God with others, reading your Bible, praying, etc.)

My Prayer and Reflection

_____

_____

_____

_____

_____

_____

_____

_____

_____

_____

_____

_____

_____

_____

_____

_____

DAY 68 — The Grace of God

Stephen, a man full of God's grace and power,
performed amazing miracles and signs among the people.
ACTS 6:8

What would it look like to be a woman full of God's grace and power? What kind of a life would you have to live? You would have to live a life full of love, a life fully devoted to and focused on God. Your life would have to be full of compassion and mercy. You would have to be bold in your faith, not for the sake of being bold, but because you just couldn't contain it. When people looked at your life, they would instantly see something different in you. Your love for others would set you apart.

In the everyday world of being a teenager, how can you show God's full love to others? It's all in your attitude. You can be full of love while walking down the hallways of your school. You can realize that no job is too small, that God is in the smallest of details as well as the bigger things in life. You can embrace who you are and where you are in this season of your life, learning and growing as you go. It's fine to not have all the answers; you should be okay with that. Right now—and for the rest of your life—is a great time to rely on the grace of God. You can trust God with every step of your life.

Father,
Thank you for the privilege and gift of life. Help me to realize I need your love in every aspect of my life. Thank you for your grace and power and love. Help me daily to pass those gifts to everyone around me. Amen.

REFLECTION QUESTIONS

1. What do you think it would look like for you to be full of grace and God's power?

2. What are some ways you can show God's full love to others?

3. What are some parts of your life where you can start showing more love and grace to others?

✑ My Prayer and Reflection ✑

_____

_____

_____

_____

_____

_____

_____

_____

_____

_____

_____

_____

_____

_____

_____

_____

_____

DAY 69 — *Going the Extra Mile*

So the Word became human and made his home among us.
He was full of unfailing love and faithfulness. And we have
seen his glory, the glory of the Father's one and only Son.
JOHN 1:14

It's so easy to blame others for their mistakes—and for our own. We do it all the time, because then we don't have to examine ourselves. We don't have to admit that we're not perfect, and we don't have to deal with the situation. But what if we stopped blaming others, even when things went wrong and it was totally their fault? What if instead of blaming others, we chose to give them grace? What if we told them that it was okay, that we weren't upset, that it wasn't a big deal? We love when grace is given to us, especially when we are so undeserving. So it should make sense for us to give that grace back to others.

Has there ever been a time in your life when you deserved to be punished, but for whatever reason, you were not? Do you remember what a great feeling that was? Maybe your debt was forgiven, or the teacher forgot the detention, or the police officer just gave you a warning for speeding. That is what grace feels like—getting a free pass.

God's grace is so much greater. He loves us even when we we're unlovable. He gives grace even when we don't notice or are unappreciative. God's grace has given us eternal life. Talk about a gift that keeps on giving! Today, choose to give grace. Stop yourself when you start to blame others, and make a conscious effort to give grace instead of judgment.

Father,
I cannot completely comprehend your endless love
because I am human, but I am so thankful that you love
and accept me the way you do. I want a loving heart like yours.
I want to always give grace. Teach me; I am willing to learn. Amen.

REFLECTION QUESTIONS

1. Why is it so hard to give grace instead of blaming someone for doing something wrong?

2. What do you think it would look like if you chose to give grace to your parents? To your friends? To your siblings? To someone you don't really like?

3. Right now, is there someone who has hurt you? What do you think would happen if you chose to give that person grace instead of judgment?

My Prayer and Reflection

_____

_____

_____

_____

_____

_____

_____

_____

_____

_____

_____

_____

_____

_____

_____

_____

_____

_____

What Do You Have to Give?

They entered the house and saw the child with his mother, Mary, and they bowed down and worshiped him. Then they opened their treasure chests and gave him gifts of gold, frankincense, and myrrh.
MATTHEW 2:11

You've probably seen a number of Christmas pageants or nativity scenes—you may have even taken part in one—but have you ever really thought about what happened at the manger? When the wise men saw Jesus, they instantly worshipped him and offered their treasures to him. Think about that for a minute. Jesus was a baby, born to a woman of no real significance in life. The wise men were Magi, priests of high social standing. Yet the wise men recognized instantly that Jesus was different; he wasn't a normal baby. And so they worshiped him, offering their gifts.

What gifts do you have to offer Jesus? Many teens may think they have nothing to give. That's not true. You have many treasures to offer Jesus. You can offer to feed his sheep (see John 21:17), which means you can share God's love with your friends, your family, the kids at your school, and anyone you meet. You can give the treasure of your time by serving others, volunteering in your church, or even taking time out of your busy schedule to talk with your family and hang out with them. You could give unconditional love to the people in your friend group and those outside of your friend group. Remember, it is not what you give; it is the heart with which you give.

Father,

Thank you for sending your only Son to be born, to live and die for me. I want to give back to you—anything and everything that I have. Like the wise men, I want to acknowledge that Jesus is Lord of all, and I want to give him what I have. Amen.

REFLECTION QUESTIONS

1. How do you think the Magi knew that the baby Jesus was different and worthy to be worshipped?

2. What would it look like for you to give your treasure to Jesus?

3. What treasure do you think you have to give? How can you give of this treasure in a way that honors God and draws others to him?

~ My Prayer and Reflection ~

_____

_____

_____

_____

_____

_____

_____

_____

_____

_____

_____

_____

_____

_____

_____

_____

_____

_____

DAY 71 — Childlike Faith

Mary responded, "I am the Lord's servant. May everything you have said about me come true." And then the angel left her.
LUKE 1:38

Mary had a tremendous amount of faith in the Lord when Gabriel visited her (Luke 1:28–38). She was a young girl, a virgin, engaged to Joseph. Gabriel, an angel sent by God, told Mary that she would give birth to the Son of God and that she would name him Jesus. How do you think you would have responded to the angel Gabriel? Would you have faith that what the angel was telling you was true? Would you argue that you were too young? Would you laugh in disbelief? Mary's response was, "I am the Lord's servant. May your word to me be fulfilled." Amazing faith for a girl who was so young; many people think she was between 13–15 years old!

What would it look like to have a childlike—yet mature—faith like Mary? What would it look like to say, "I am the Lord's servant"? Obviously, God is not asking you to give birth to his Son, but he does ask that you love all of his children, including people you don't like. God also calls us to honor our mother and father, which can be really hard when we disagree with them or don't want to always follow their rules. And God asks us to forgive seventy times seven (Matthew 18:22), which sounds like a whole lot of forgiveness. There are certain hard things God asks of all of us, and when we obey we will be blessed by our obedience. It takes having a childlike faith to obey without asking questions—a faith like Mary had.

Father,

I look at Mary, and I feel like I'm so far away from having that kind of blind, childlike faith that makes me willing to do whatever you ask of me. But I want that kind of faith. I want to do whatever you ask of me. Help me take one step of obedience at a time. Amen.

152

REFLECTION QUESTIONS

1. If you were to have the kind of faith Mary had, what would that look like for you?

2. Has God ever asked you to do something that was hard for you to accept? How did you respond to God? What happened?

3. What makes it hard for you to have great faith? Why is it important?

My Prayer and Reflection

_____

_____

_____

_____

_____

_____

_____

_____

_____

_____

_____

_____

_____

_____

_____

_____

_____

Be Rooted

> *But blessed are those who trust in the LORD and have made the LORD their hope and confidence. They are like trees planted along a riverbank, with roots that reach deep into the water. Such trees are not bothered by the heat or worried by long months of drought. Their leaves stay green, and they never stop producing fruit.*
> JEREMIAH 17:7–8

We are always putting our confidence and trust in something. How many times have you placed your confidence in someone or something only to be disappointed? You can place your trust in someone only to find out they betrayed you. You can put your confidence and trust in having a boyfriend, but then you break up. You can put your confidence and trust in having a perfect GPA, but then you get a B+ in a class. You can put your confidence and trust in your parent's marriage, but then they get a divorce. Being popular, being athletic, being pretty, being artistically or musically talented—we think these things give us value, but we shouldn't be rooted in these things. We should be rooted in God.

God blesses those who put their confidence and trust in him. God blesses those who say, "I'm all in, no matter what!" This type of confidence in God is unmistakable, not because of your declaration, but because of your actions. When you trust in God with all your heart, there is no denying God's presence in your life. When something is taken away from you, you are able to stay calm because you have learned to trust in God and not in your circumstances. You have remained rooted in God.

Father,

You are faithful. You are worthy of my trust, and I pray that I would put all my confidence in you. God, I want my life to reflect you in all things—in the good and bad times. I know a drought will come, but keep me close to and rooted in you, and I will make it through. Amen.

REFLECTION QUESTIONS

1. Right now, where are you placing your confidence and trust?

2. When disappointment comes and your trust is broken, how do you react?

3. What can you do to start trusting more in God and placing all your confidence in him?

 *My Prayer and Reflection*

Daily Reliance

First, help me never to tell a lie. Second, give me neither poverty nor riches! Give me just enough to satisfy my needs. For if I grow rich, I may deny you and say, "Who is the LORD?" And if I am too poor, I may steal and thus insult God's holy name.

PROVERBS 30:8–9

Do you find that your prayers are often more like a list of things you're asking God for? Don't worry—you're not alone. From things you don't need (an expensive bag, trendy jeans or shoes) to things you do need (nicer friends, better focus when you study), we're told to bring all of our requests to God. But he also wants us to ask for "just enough" to satisfy our needs. That's because relying on God for our daily bread keeps us dependent on him, and that is where we need to be. We should be dependent on God for material things like food and clothing, as well as wisdom, love for others, and good relationships. We need to depend on God for *everything* in our lives.

God knows our human nature. He knows that the more we have, the less we will look to him to meet our needs. That's why in the Bible, God only gave the Israelites manna—the food they relied on to survive—one day at a time, to keep them dependent on him. God doesn't want us to look too far into the future. Instead, he wants us to keep our eyes focused on the here and now and on his provision. He will care of your future. He knows what you need each day.

Father,

Thank you for my daily bread. I pray that I would rely on you for all things. I ask that you would teach me how to become less dependent on material things and the things that this world values and more dependent on you. Amen.

REFLECTION QUESTIONS

1. When everyone around seems like they have "more" of everything than you have, how do you feel? How do you think you could learn to be content with what you have?

2. What do you think it means to rely daily on God? What would this look like in your life?

3. It's not wrong to want "more"—we can't help it sometimes. But how can you keep it balanced with being dependent on God?

୧୭ My Prayer and Reflection ୧୭

_____

_____

_____

_____

_____

_____

_____

_____

_____

_____

_____

_____

_____

_____

_____

_____

_____

_____

God's Strength

*I pray that from his glorious, unlimited resources he will empower
you with inner strength through his Spirit. Then Christ will make
his home in your hearts as you trust in him. Your roots
will grow down into God's love and keep you strong.*

EPHESIANS 3:16–17

We need the strength of God daily in our lives. Life is too stressful to tackle it by ourselves; we need the help of our heavenly Father. Life demands a lot from you—being accepted and part of a good friend group, dealing with the pressure to perform and be the best, keeping your behavior always in check. It's a lot! Life is too hard to do on your own. If we do not look to God to fill us up, give us love and acceptance, and help us through the hard times, eventually we will be empty inside.

God doesn't want you to be hollow inside or a slave to the demands of this world. He loves you and wants to empower you with his strength. He doesn't want you to live your life stressed out, anxious, and worrying. Are you receiving the help that God is freely giving you? Or are you trying to do life in your own strength? Take advantage of the gift that God is offering you in his strength; you will never regret it.

Father,
*Thank you for your Spirit that gives me strength.
I need your strength. I am weary, empty, tired, and
I need you! Fill me up from my innermost being to the point
of overflowing. I thank you for this amazing gift. Amen.*

REFLECTION QUESTIONS

1. When do you tend to feel stressed out and overwhelmed in your life?

2. How do you handle your stress and anxiety?

3. What do you think would happen if you involved God and asked him to relieve your stress and give you his strength?

✑ My Prayer and Reflection ✑

_____

_____

_____

_____

_____

_____

_____

_____

_____

_____

_____

_____

_____

_____

_____

_____

_____

_____

Everlasting Love

And this hope will not lead to disappointment.
For we know how dearly God loves us, because he has
given us the Holy Spirit to fill our hearts with his love.
ROMANS 5:5

Some days we just feel good about ourselves and our life. On these days, love pours out like a faucet onto our friends and family. Other days, we haven't even gotten through our first class of the day, and we feel like the day will never end with all the annoying people who are surrounding us and all the things that are going wrong. But don't be discouraged; Jesus gave us the gift of the Holy Spirit. The Holy Spirit is full of grace, patience, and everlasting love—and he has more than enough to share with us.

God loves us so much that he sent us his Son. When Jesus ascended into heaven, God's love for us did not stop; he sent us the Holy Spirit. Through the Holy Spirit, we have God's love in us, which is all the love we will ever need to survive our days. So, on those days when you feel that you will not be able to love the people in your life unconditionally, lean into the Holy Spirit and ask him to fill you with his love. Be honest! Tell God, "I'm ready to give up on this relationship, but I know I need to love them. God, I can't do that without you, without your Holy Spirit." God will meet you where you are and give you his everlasting love to share with others.

Father,

Thank you for the gift of the Holy Spirit. I admit I don't
always understand how the Trinity works, but I trust you.
I know you gave us the Holy Spirit to comfort us, to guide us,
and to fill us with what we need when we need it. Help me to
remember this on days when I just don't feel very loving. Amen.

REFLECTION QUESTIONS

1. What type of people are the hardest for you to love?

2. What do you think it would look like if God truly gave you an amazing love for even the most difficult people in your life?

3. What are your trigger points with certain people? How can God's everlasting love for you help you to show love to them?

My Prayer and Reflection

_____

_____

_____

_____

_____

_____

_____

_____

_____

_____

_____

_____

_____

_____

_____

_____

_____

Live Every Day on Purpose

*Plant your seed in the morning and keep
busy all afternoon, for you don't know if profit will
come from one activity or another—or maybe both.*
ECCLESIASTES 11:6

Have you ever noticed that when you are bored, that's when you tend to focus on yourself and you're most likely to let anxiety and negative thoughts creep into your head? You might start comparing yourself to others and become full of self-pity, experience feelings of depression, or obsess over certain thoughts and ideas that aren't healthy to think about. The opposite of being bored is keeping busy. The moment your feet hit the floor when you get out of bed, thank God for the day ahead of you. Ask him what he has in store for you today. Think about who you could be a warm hug to. Start living every day on purpose—and *with* purpose.

One way to keep your mind busy is to do things for others. When you are serving, helping, and thinking of others, you don't have time to dwell on yourself. Plant good seeds—and good deeds—throughout your day. Could you offer a helpful hand to your mom? What nice thing could you do for your friends and classmates at school? Even something as simple as telling your teacher that she is doing a good job at teaching could brighten her day. Are there clubs in your school that need your help? You can also volunteer at church on Sundays or during the week. Most people and groups are in need of some help; you just have to look around and ask. If you can't think of anyone to help, what about your grandparents? You could call them, stop by and visit them in person, or send them an old-fashioned letter letting them know how you are doing and asking about them. These little gestures will make a world of difference to so many people, including you. Don't worry how your seeds of helping others will grow and bloom; just scatter them about and let God do the rest.

Father,

*Please show me how and where I can be helpful to those around me.
Help me to start to look at this world through a different lens and not
be so self-consumed. Bless me in my endeavors and my willingness to
want to help others. Let me live every day on purpose for you. Amen.*

REFLECTION QUESTIONS

1. A lot of times we do things to get credit for them, or to get attention for ourselves in some way, but the verse in Ecclesiastes suggests that we plant our seeds even if we don't know what the result will be. What does that mean to you?

2. How do you think you can you do a better job of living with purpose?

3. God is in charge of the seeds that grow and bloom, not us. Does that idea give you relief and comfort that the pressure is off of you, or do you want the credit? Explain.

My Prayer and Reflection

_____

_____

_____

_____

_____

_____

_____

_____

_____

_____

_____

_____

_____

_____

_____

_____

_____

_____

_____

Who Are You Pleasing?

*Obviously, I'm not trying to win the approval
of people, but of God. If pleasing people
were my goal, I would not be Christ's servant.*
GALATIANS 1:10

It is so easy to look to other people and do things to try and please them. Think about it. We all want to be liked, we all want to be accepted, and we all want to be a part of something. Therefore, we do things to please others. We go along with the latest trends because that is what our friends are doing. We might agree to do something that we know isn't really good for us, but we do it to please others. We say yes to too many things because we're afraid someone will be upset with us if we say no. Our need to fit in and belong is BIG. A lot of the time, we equate pleasing others with being loved and accepted. But the truth is that in God, we are *already* loved and accepted.

To be liked and accepted by our peers—and everyone around us—is a big deal, and it's something that is naturally important to us. We want to be included, not excluded. But often we live our lives trying to please the people around us, completely forgetting about pleasing the one who truly matters—God. This week, try to keep God front and center in your thoughts. Before you say yes to someone, run the idea by God and ask him what his opinion is. Before you do something just because someone else did it, pray and ask God what he thinks you should do. Ask yourself, *Who am I pleasing?* You truly only need the approval of one person, and that is God.

Father,

*Thank you for loving me and being patient with me. Help me to
remember that I only have to please you in my life—everything
and everyone else is just a bonus. Give me wisdom as I live
my day-to-day life. I pray I will glorify you in all that I do. Amen.*

REFLECTION QUESTIONS

1. Who do you try to please the most in your life? Why do you think you need the approval of this person or these people?

2. Is it hard to think about pleasing God? Why or why not?

3. How can you start living your life so you're more focused on God's approval than on the approval of others?

⸎ My Prayer and Reflection ⸎

_____

_____

_____

_____

_____

_____

_____

_____

_____

_____

_____

_____

_____

_____

_____

_____

_____

Leave Justice to God

*The Lord gives righteousness and
justice to all who are treated unfairly.*
PSALM 103:6

Life doesn't feel fair a lot of the time. When my daughters were in high school, they would tell me about friends of theirs who would cheat on tests to get good grades. I, of course, told them that cheating was wrong and that they did not need to cheat, but instead they should study for their tests and do the hard work. One statement I would hear over and over from all of my girls was, "Life doesn't seem fair!" I would agree with them that life is not fair at times. Their friends never got caught cheating, and they succeeded in all they did without any type of punishment, which is definitely not fair.

The thing we have to keep in mind is that God is the one who will judge in the end, and he will make everything right. He sees you doing what is right, even if no one else does. He sees that you are not lying to your teacher or parents. He sees that you are not cheating. He sees that you are making wise decisions even when it is hard, and he will make sure you are rewarded. Remember that God is in it for the long haul. You may not see justice with your friends while you are in school, but he is in control. God sees all. And he never rewards cheating or any type of disobedience. When life doesn't seem fair, trust in what the Bible says: "The Lord gives righteousness and justice to all who are treated unfairly."

Father,

*Thank you for loving me. Thank you for always seeing everything
and for making justice happen, even if it seems to take a long time.
Help me to trust in you and to make wise decisions. Help me to
do what is right, no matter what the circumstances are. Amen.*

REFLECTION QUESTIONS

1. What is a situation you've been through recently when life didn't seem fair? How did you feel about this situation (helpless, angry, frustrated)?

2. How do you feel knowing that God will bring justice in the end?

3. Is it easy for you to trust God with the unfairness of life? Why or why not?

 *My Prayer and Reflection*

_____

_____

_____

_____

_____

_____

_____

_____

_____

_____

_____

_____

_____

_____

_____

_____

_____

_____

_____

_____

It Starts with Doubt

*The serpent was the shrewdest of all the wild animals the L*ord *God had made. One day he asked the woman, "Did God really say you must not eat the fruit from any of the trees in the garden?"*

GENESIS 3:1

God created a beautiful, perfect world for Adam and Eve. He only gave them one rule and that was not to eat of the "fruit from the tree in the middle of the garden" (Genesis 3:2). A simple rule really, not a hard one to follow. But the serpent, who was Satan, had a plan to place doubt in the mind of Eve to get her to disobey God's one rule. When you read Genesis 3, you see clearly that Eve knew exactly what God said. But the serpent placed doubt in her mind when he said, "Did God *really* say that?" Have you ever heard Satan ask you that same type of question? He usually says it so innocently: "Is that *really* wrong?" or "Where in the Bible does it say *not* to do this thing?" Satan throws those questions out to us so innocently, yet he knows exactly what he is doing. He is trying to get us to fall. When we take the bait and listen to him, he will turn on us and fill us with shame and guilt for doing the wrong thing. And it all starts when we doubt ourselves.

Satan's goal is to keep us away from God and God's will for our life. Where God wants to give us a life full of joy and peace, Satan wants to give us a life of sadness and misery. His goal is to get us to fall, like he did with Eve. Jesus tell us that Satan is the author of all lies, but that Jesus is the truth (John 8:44; John 14:6). Make sure you pay attention to who you are listening to. Does that voice in your mind come from God, or is it coming from somewhere else? If you doubt that something is coming from God, it's probably not. Stay close to Jesus, and stay aware.

Father,

Please open my eyes so I can distinguish your voice from the enemy's voice. I want to listen to truth, not lies. I know that in order for me to know your truth, I must read your word. Give me a desire to want to read the Bible and to understand what it is saying. Also give me the desire to pray more and stay connected to you so I won't have so much doubt in my mind. Amen.

REFLECTION QUESTIONS

1. Has there ever been a time in your life when you could hear Satan telling you lies? What was he telling you, and what happened?

2. Why do you think it can be so hard to know what is right and what is wrong? Why do you think having doubt messes up our lives so much?

3. How do you think knowing the truth of Jesus can change the way you choose to live your life?

My Prayer and Reflection

_____

_____

_____

_____

_____

_____

_____

_____

_____

_____

_____

_____

_____

_____

_____

_____

_____

_____

_____

Truth Matters

And you will know the truth, and the truth will set you free.
JOHN 8:32

We live in a world where it seems like there are no real truths anymore. There are no absolutes. We're told that whatever you feel or believe is good, and whatever I feel and believe is good. While this might sound nice, Jesus said that there *are* absolute truths in the world. For instance, he said that there is one true God who is eternal, which means he is never-ending. Another truth God gave us is the Trinity—the Father, the Son, and the Holy Spirit. We also are given the truth that Jesus came to earth, born of a virgin, and that he was crucified, buried, and resurrected after three days. He died for our sins, to be the bridge that connects us, a sinful people, to a Holy God. God also gives us the truth that the Holy Spirit was sent after Jesus left the earth to remain with us, to be our counselor, our comforter, and our power. These truths matter, because there is only one way to get to the Father, and that is through his Son, Jesus.

Jesus said that the truth will set you free. He is the truth! In him, you can be free of your pain, free of your guilt, free of your shame, free of your sin, free of your bondage. In him, you are set free, and you can have a life full of joy and peace, regardless of your circumstances. The good news is that you don't have to worry about sorting out what's true and what's not—God already did that for you. Just know that the truth matters and that God will show you the truth when you read his word and stay close to him.

Father,

Thank you for showing me your truth throughout the Bible. It comforts me to know that there are truths that I can count on and hold on to. When I doubt and get confused about what's true and what's not, show me the way back to you and your truth. Make your word real to me. Amen.

REFLECTION QUESTIONS

1. Do you struggle with absolute truths? Why or why not?

2. Jesus said, "The truth will set you free." What does that mean to you? What are some things you're wondering about? What does God say about these things in his Word?

My Prayer and Reflection

_____

_____

_____

_____

_____

_____

_____

_____

_____

_____

_____

_____

_____

_____

_____

_____

_____

_____

_____

_____

Walk in Truth

Some of the traveling teachers recently returned and made me very happy by telling me about your faithfulness and that you are living according to the truth. I could have no greater joy than to hear that my children are following the truth.

3 JOHN 3-4

What do you think someone would write about if they were to follow you through your daily life and write about it—your conversations with other people, the things you did, how you reacted to certain situations? You might not want anyone to read your life story—especially on certain days—but fortunately, people wrote about Jesus. Because they wrote about his daily life, we can discover more about who he is and how he lived his life. One of those writers, John, walked with Jesus and saw him perform many miracles. John saw Jesus crucified, buried, and resurrected, and he saw Jesus after Jesus rose from the dead. John believed that Jesus was the Son of God. This kind of belief is not shaken, and John devoted the rest of his life to telling others about Jesus and walking in God's truth.

It is important that we believe in Jesus, but it is also important that we follow the truth of God. That is where real life change happens. When you say you believe that Jesus is the Son of God and died for your sins, that is wonderful! But when you take it to the next level and say, "Because I believe, I will follow him and follow his truth," that will set you apart. You will start experiencing a richer life with Jesus. Walking in truth is the best way to live your life. And even if nobody is recording the story of your life, you're still making an impression on others. Make sure it's a good one!

Father,

I want to not just believe your truth but also to walk in your truth. I want to know you personally and intimately. I want your thoughts to be my thoughts, your ways to be my ways. Teach me how to walk in your truth. Amen.

REFLECTION QUESTIONS

1. When you're in school and around your friends, is it hard for you to stay true to your beliefs? Why or why not?

2. In what areas do you most struggle to walk in truth?

3. How do you think God can help you stay strong in your beliefs, even around people who aren't walking in truth?

∽ My Prayer and Reflection ∾

_____

_____

_____

_____

_____

_____

_____

_____

_____

_____

_____

_____

_____

_____

_____

_____

_____

_____

Love the Truth

*He will use every kind of evil deception to fool those
on their way to destruction, because they refuse
to love and accept the truth that would save them.*
2 THESSALONIANS 2:10

The plot of a lot of movies can be boiled down to one thing: the bad guys versus the good guys. Movies like this are so popular because they reflect what's actually true in this world. We have an enemy, and his name is Satan. You might not want to hear this, but he has a mission—to kill and destroy (John 10:10). Here's what you do want to hear: Jesus also has a mission—to give life and give it to us in full (John 10:10). It is important that we as Christians know and understand these two missions, one of good and one of evil. In this world there are two realms—the realm of God, which is good, and the realm of Satan, which is evil. Everything falls into one of those realms. This truth is not to scare us, but to educate us so that we will know how to live our lives. Here's how the story ends: Jesus wins! Jesus conquers all evil in the end.

We must know that Jesus is the way, the truth, and life, so we *know* truth. We must also *walk* after the truth. Daily, we need to make a conscious effort to walk with Jesus, and we must also *love* the truth. To love the truth means that we trust what Jesus says is true and we understand that he wants good for us. We, in turn, love his truth because it is good for us. Truth wins. Jesus wins. And we want to be on the winning side.

Father,

*I am learning the difference between good and evil, and I will not
be afraid. You are my protector. In you I have a safe place to hide.
Teach me your truth, as I want to know it, walk in it, and love it. Amen.*

REFLECTION QUESTIONS

1. When it comes to truth, do you have a hard time believing God's truth? Why or why not?

2. If you truly trusted God and his Word, how do you think that would that change your life?

3. How do you think believing God and what he says is true would help with fear, anxiety, or depression?

My Prayer and Reflection

_____

_____

_____

_____

_____

_____

_____

_____

_____

_____

_____

_____

_____

_____

_____

_____

_____

_____

_____

I Will Look to the Lord

Search for the LORD and for His strength; continually seek him.
1 CHRONICLES 16:11

Life can feel overwhelming at times. Have you ever wondered why life won't give you a break, why the hits just seem to keep coming? We can feel like we are way out in the ocean and wave after wave keeps knocking us down, not giving us a chance to get up. That is what life can be like. These pounding waves can come in all forms—fights with your friends, clashes you're your teachers or coaches, boyfriend drama, family problems like divorce or arguing, struggles with your schoolwork, even world events that affect you and cause you to have anxiety about the future.

When life is giving you a beating, always remember to look to the Lord for your strength. Call out to him and ask him to hold you up, to help you stand strong against the force that is pounding you. The Creator of the Universe—the almighty God, the one true God—is on your side. You are his child. He wants to hear from you, to listen to your worries and concerns. Ask him to give you the strength to conquer life and to get through the battles you are experiencing. When you're being pounded by the waves of life, look to God and you will find the strength you need to make it through.

Father,

Give me your strength. I know you are on my side, and you want to help me through my hard circumstances. Give me the strength to know what to do with my friend drama, with my family issues, with my school pressures, and with anything else I am going through. In you, I can triumph, but I need your strength. Thank you for giving it to me. Amen.

REFLECTION QUESTIONS

1. What tough situation are you in right now that is making you feel like you're getting hit with one wave after another?

2. How do you think God's strength could help you through this time in your life?

3. Do you think that there is any problem too big for God? Why or why not?

ℰ𝒶 My Prayer and Reflection ᘓ

_____

_____

_____

_____

_____

_____

_____

_____

_____

_____

_____

_____

_____

_____

_____

_____

You Are Worthy

*But God showed his great love for us by sending
Christ to die for us while we were still sinners.*

ROMANS 5:8

You are deeply loved by your heavenly Father. Don't ever forget that. No matter how you "feel," always know that you are loved. You do not have to perform a certain way. You do not have to be good all the time. God loves and accepts you just as you are. He also knows the true you. He knows your talents, your anger issues, your insecurities, and your deepest desires. God knows *everything* about you, and he loves all of you. We know this fact is true because God sent his Son, Jesus, to die for you, and the rest of humankind, even when we were full of sin. God accepted us even while we were sinners. We don't have to prove ourselves to him; we have already been accepted. We are worthy of his love.

The next time you feel like you're not "good enough,"—when you're comparing yourself to someone else, when someone criticizes you, when you feel like you can't say or do anything right—remind yourself you are loved and you are worthy to be loved. Whatever sins you have committed, God has forgiven you and loves you with an unconditional love—always.

Father,

Thank you for your unconditional love for me. Thank you that I don't have to perform or prove my worth to you, but that you accept me just the way I am. I am truly humbled by your love, and I want to love others and accept them the way you love and accept me. Amen.

REFLECTION QUESTIONS

1. What is the true you? Make a list of your strengths and weakness—and be honest about them.

2. Since God knows the true you, including everything listed above, do you think you can accept his unconditional love? If not, what is holding you back?

3. How do you think accepting God's unconditional love would make a difference in your life?

My Prayer and Reflection

_____

_____

_____

_____

_____

_____

_____

_____

_____

_____

_____

_____

_____

_____

_____

_____

_____

God's Peace

*I am leaving you with a gift—peace of mind
and heart. And the peace I give is a gift the
world cannot give. So don't be troubled or afraid.*
JOHN 14:27

It is easy to get caught up into the lie that in order for us to be "okay" or at peace, everyone around us must be okay. Unfortunately, life doesn't work that way all the time. The truth is, we can be okay—even when turmoil and chaos are all around us. God is always with us. Our peace comes from him, not our circumstances. For instance, your parents maybe going through hard times with each other, but God will get you through those difficult days. You may be struggling in your friendships and people may have turned their backs on you, but God is always with you. He will be your safe place even when everyone else has abandoned you. You might be struggling with your sports team and feel like your performance isn't where it should be and that your teammates and coaches are not happy with you. But God understands that you are trying your best, and he is with you.

God isn't necessarily going to change your circumstances. Of course, he might do that, but he might not. You may have to still walk through the difficult situations, but he will stay with you and give you his peace. And God's peace is everlasting. Lean into God and trust him. Accept his steadfastness even though your circumstances are anything but stable. God is with you, and with him you have peace.

Father,

*Thank you for your love and compassion for my life.
Thank you for meeting me exactly where I am with no expectations
from me. When my world feels like it is unraveling, you are with me.
When I feel all alone, you are holding me in your arms. Help me
to feel your presence and to experience your peace. Amen.*

REFLECTION QUESTIONS

1. What areas of your life feel chaotic right now?

2. How does an unstable situation make you feel? How do you tend to react when things are going wrong?

3. What do you think it would look like for you to trust in God and accept his peace?

 *My Prayer and Reflection*

_____

_____

_____

_____

_____

_____

_____

_____

_____

_____

_____

_____

_____

_____

_____

_____

_____

Pride Isn't Good

Pride leads to disgrace, but with humility comes wisdom.
PROVERBS 11:2

The mindset of entitlement is rampant in our culture. It is the mindset we have when we think, "You owe me." The truth is, no one "owes" us anything. Our parents don't owe us, our teachers don't owe us, our friends don't owe us, our coaches don't owe us, and even our church doesn't owe us. Jesus, even though he was the Son of God, didn't have a mindset of entitlement. He humbled himself and came to earth in the form of a baby to one day die on a cross to pay for our sins. There was absolutely no entitlement involved. Entitlement is a form of pride, and God says, "Pride comes before the fall" (Proverbs 16:18).

As you go about your life, you will more than likely be tempted to develop this mindset of "you owe me," but try to resist it. When you are talking with your mom and she hasn't done your laundry, resist thinking, "You owe me my laundry." When you are talking with your friends and they didn't say your outfit looks good, try to give them grace and realize they don't "owe you" any such compliment. When you get an 88 on your test and the teacher won't bump your grade to a 90, try to resist the idea that the teacher "owes you" and could just bump your grade up to a 90. Instead, accept your grade with humility and move on in life. Fight against having a mindset of entitlement. Lose the pride. Remember, the reward of humility is wisdom.

Father,

Pride is as natural to me as the air that I breathe. Show me ways where my pride is getting in my way. Help me to remember that no one owes me anything. Teach me how to live a humble life, never expecting anything from anyone. Amen.

REFLECTION QUESTIONS

1. What is your definition of entitlement? Where do you see examples of entitlement in the world today?

2. What are some areas where you struggle with entitlement?

3. How can God help you humble yourself when you realize you're acting proud or entitled?

∾ My Prayer and Reflection ∾

_____

_____

_____

_____

_____

_____

_____

_____

_____

_____

_____

_____

_____

_____

_____

_____

_____

Just as You Are

When God our Savior revealed his kindness and love, he saved us, not because of the righteous things we had done, but because of his mercy. He washed away our sins, giving us a new birth and new life through the Holy Spirit. He generously poured out the Spirit upon us through Jesus Christ our Savior.

TITUS 3:4-5

In a performance-driven world, God accepts and loves us just the way we are. We don't have to do anything to please God. We don't have to have a perfect GPA. We don't have to have a certain number of followers on social media. We don't have to be the first-chair trumpet player or the star of the school musical or the captain and MVP of the softball team. We are already loved, already accepted, already forgiven. What a breath of fresh air! Can you think of the last time when no one expected anything from you but just gave you unconditional love? You don't have to perform your way into God's heart—you are already there.

God loves you just as you are. And there's nothing you can do to make him love you more. You don't have to get perfect grades or get into a prestigious college. You don't have to be in the most popular group at school or be the best runner or cheerleader or the best anything. You can just be yourself, and God loves you exactly that way. Your performance in life has nothing to do with your being accepted by God. He loves and accepts you just as you are.

Father,

I feel like in every part of my life, my performance is being judged and evaluated. I feel like I am constantly trying to hit the mark and be the best, and it is exhausting. God, thank you for loving and accepting me just the way I am. Amen.

REFLECTION QUESTIONS

1. In what parts of your life do you feel the most pressure to perform?

2. How does this performance-driven mentality make you feel?

3. How do you feel knowing that God accepts you just as you are? How does this help you to accept yourself?

My Prayer and Reflection

_____

_____

_____

_____

_____

_____

_____

_____

_____

_____

_____

_____

_____

_____

_____

_____

Happiness Is Tied to God

*I know the LORD is always with me. I will not
be shaken, for he is right beside me. No wonder my
heart is glad, and I rejoice. My body rests in safety.*
PSALM 16:8-9

Many times in life we say, "I would be happy if _____." Fill in your blank. It could be: if I had a boyfriend; if my parents were still married; if I had nicer clothes; if I had a car to drive; if I were popular; if I were good at sports; if I were talented in dance, art, or anything. We can dream our lives away wishing for things we don't have and convincing ourselves that if we had them, everything would be better. But true happiness doesn't come from any of those things.

True happiness comes from within, and it is not dependent on what we have or what our circumstances are in life. When God is at the center of our lives, that is when we are the happiest of all. Material things can leave us wanting more. You might have a lot of clothes, but trends are always changing—so you keep wanting more clothes. You might have a car, but it eventually gets old and starts needing more and more work—so you want a new car. You might have a boyfriend now, but one of you might start liking someone else—so you break up and you start looking for another relationship. Everything that can bring us happiness in this world depends on something else.

Place God in the center of your life, and build your happiness around him. A wish list isn't a bad thing, but if you feel like you will only be happy if you get everything on your list, you'll never find true happiness. No material item, relationship, or prestige can truly make you happy. If you tie your happiness to God, though, you'll discover what it means to be truly happy.

Father,
I pray that I will keep you front and center in my life always.
God, when I start to veer off course, gently remind me that you
are the source of my true happiness. I know it is normal to want
certain things in my life, but always draw me back to you. Amen.

REFLECTION QUESTIONS

1. How would you fill in the blank: "I would be happy if _____"?

2. What makes you think your answer would make you happy?

3. What if you released control of your blank space and gave it to God? What do you think would happen?

My Prayer and Reflection

No Shame

*He personally carried our sins in his body on
the cross so that we can be dead to sin and live
for what is right. By his wounds you are healed you.*
1 PETER 2:24

Do you ever feel judged by others? Like you disappointed the people around you by not doing what they thought you were capable of? Like you made one tiny mistake, and now people think you can't do anything right? Whether it's a minor embarrassing moment or a major mistake, we play those scenes over and over in our minds—and we assume that other people do too. Some of the best news about being a Christian is there is no condemnation in Jesus Christ (Romans 8:1). This means that when God looks at us, he does not see our sin, our selfishness, our pride, or our mistakes. He only sees his Son, Jesus, who died on the cross for our sins. What an amazing gift! This means we can walk free with our heads held high and walk in God's perfect love. We do not need to live in shame for the things we've done. Our sins have been forgiven.

The next time Satan whispers in your ear that you are not worthy because of what you have done or you aren't good enough or that you don't measure up, resist his lies and say out loud, "There is no condemnation in Jesus Christ." Through the wounds of Jesus, we are healed from shame, healed from guilt, healed from our sins. Don't let the enemy get away with his lies. Remember, Jesus described Satan as the father of lies (John 8: 44). God loves you, God is proud of you, and God forgives you when you mess up. In him there is no shame.

Father,

*Thank you for your Son, Jesus. Thank you that his blood covers
all of my sin and that in him I am accepted and loved by you.
God, I don't deserve such a gift, but I will gladly accept it.
Please help me not to obsess about my mistakes, big or small.
Thank you that there is no shame in a life lived for you. Amen.*

REFLECTION QUESTIONS

1. What things in your life bring you guilt and shame?

2. What does it mean to you that there is no condemnation in Christ Jesus?

3. How does it make you feel knowing that Jesus already paid the price for your sin?

∽ My Prayer and Reflection ∾

_____

_____

_____

_____

_____

_____

_____

_____

_____

_____

_____

_____

_____

_____

_____

_____

_____

_____

God Is Your Helper

So let us come boldly to the throne of our gracious God. There we will receive his mercy, and we will find grace to help us when we need it most.

HEBREWS 4:16

Many times in our lives, we just need a little help. A little help with the math problem or chemistry equation. A little help on the soccer or softball field. A little help in our relationships with our friends or our boyfriend. A little help navigating the changing relationship we have with our parents as we get older. If you could press a "help" button and someone would magically appear to give you the help you needed, wouldn't that be nice?

Actually, we *can* press that "help" button and ask for help from the Creator of the Universe, God. And he will give us the help we need, right when we need it. Because Jesus died on the cross for our sins, he built a bridge that directly connects us to God. No longer do you have to go through someone to talk to God. You have direct access to the almighty God every day. Hebrews 4:16 tells us that we can go with complete trust to the throne of God. (Other translations use the word *confidence* instead of *trust*.) We can enter into God's presence with confidence, knowing that he is there for us and will listen to our requests. He is ready and willing to give us all the help and wisdom we need. We just have to press the "help" button and ask.

Father,

What a blessing to have a direct connection to you through Jesus. Help me trust you more every day, God, and help me to put my complete and total faith in you. You are my helper! God, I look to you to meet my needs, knowing that only you can fully do that. Amen.

REFLECTION QUESTIONS

1. What is your definition of confidence?

2. What does it mean to you to have confidence or trust in another person? How do you feel knowing that you can completely trust God and that he will be there for you?

3. If you could push the "help" button right now, in what area of your life would you ask for that help? How do you think God will help you?

My Prayer and Reflection

God Can Handle It

*Dear friends, never take revenge. Leave that to the righteous anger of God. For the Scriptures say, "I will take revenge; I will pay them back," says the L*ORD.

ROMANS 12:19

When we are wronged by others, whether it be our parents, friends, teachers, coaches, teammates, classmates, or anyone else, our natural tendency is to want to take matters into our own hands and get revenge. We go over and over the situation in our minds and think through all the possible ways we can get back at the person who hurt us. No one likes to treated unfairly or to be taken advantage of. No one likes to be called out, disciplined, or humiliated—especially in front of other people. We want to get back at the person, to make things right, to make ourselves look good again, but God tells us to leave the revenge to him. He is the perfect judge, and he will bring justice.

The problem happens, however, when God's timing doesn't line up with our timing. We want justice *right now*. But God isn't in the business of always acting immediately; sometimes he plays the long game. His ultimate goal is to bring even our enemies into a relationship with himself. And he may be using this instance to do just that. God gives all of us the opportunity to choose him, but in the end he will have justice. In the meantime, put your trust in God, and let him deal with the people who seem like they're against you. Don't seek revenge. Allow God to handle it. You will be happier in the end, and you never know who might come to know the Lord.

Father,

Many times when I am wronged, I want to take matters into my own hands. I've never really thought about you taking that challenge on for me. Thank you. The next time someone is against me, please remind me that you are my avenger and my protector. Help me to trust in you. Amen.

REFLECTION QUESTIONS

1. At what times do you most want to seek revenge?

2. What is it in you that wants revenge?

3. What do you think it would it look like to allow God to avenge you? How do you think this would change how you interacted with others?

⨋ My Prayer and Reflection ⨋

You Are a Conqueror in Christ

No, despite all these things, overwhelming victory is ours through Christ, who loved us.
ROMANS 8:37

Let's talk a little more about the topic of yesterday's devotional—what to do when someone has wronged you. When you feel mistreated or taken advantage of in life, it is easy to feel like the victim. When a friend turns their back on you and you feel completely rejected. When you've been accused of something you didn't do and no one is believing your side of the story. When your coach never plays you and you sit on the bench game after game. In these moments, it is easy to start believing you are the victim and that life is not fair. When you're in these situations, keep in mind that God will go before you and fight your battles for you—you just need to trust in him. Also, remember that in Jesus Christ you are never a victim; he is your conqueror. And because you are his follower, that makes you a conqueror too.

In Jesus, you have power over all things. Through Jesus' shed blood on the cross, you have his power in you. You have the power to be strong and courageous when your friends mistreat you. You have the power to trust God that the truth will be brought to light when no one is believing you. You have the power to persevere and keep doing your best and working hard in practice even if the coach doesn't play you. God promises to work all things together for his good (Romans 8:28). This means that you are not a victim, but a conqueror in Christ.

Father,

In Christ Jesus I am a conqueror over all who mistreat me or make things unfair for me. I never want to fall into the victim mindset, because then I will feel sorry for myself, which is never good. Help me to remember who I am in Christ and that your love for me will get me through any hard circumstances. Amen.

REFLECTION QUESTIONS

1. What does being a conqueror mean to you?

2. Do you tend to feel more like a victim or a conqueror in life? Why do you think you feel this way?

3. What do you think it would look like if you allowed Jesus' power to infiltrate your life? How do you think he could help you?

My Prayer and Reflection

_____

_____

_____

_____

_____

_____

_____

_____

_____

_____

_____

_____

_____

_____

_____

_____

DAY 93

You Are Chosen

You are coming to Christ, who is the living cornerstone of God's temple. He was rejected by people, but he was chosen by God for great honor. And you are the living stones that God is building into his spiritual temple. What's more, you are his holy priests. Through the mediation of Jesus Christ, you offer spiritual sacrifices that please God.

1 PETER 2:4-5

Do you ever feel rejected by your peers? Do you feel the loneliness of walking into the cafeteria and not seeing anyone you know and stressing out about where to sit? Have you ever been the only one in your friend group who was *not* invited to the party? Have you spent time scrolling on social media, looking at all the fun stuff everyone else is doing—stuff that nobody told you about? It's not a great feeling to be rejected or left out. It's easy to feel like you are invisible or like nobody wants you around. But know that you *are* seen and wanted and loved. Take hope, because God has chosen you, and you are always welcome to hang out with him.

Jesus knew exactly what it was like to feel rejected when he was here on earth. He has been where you are. He knows what it's like to have people whisper about you, make fun of you (both behind your back and to your face), and spread rumors about you. He really gets it. You are not alone now—or ever—because Jesus is with you. Even if you can't feel him, he is there. Know that you are loved and chosen by him, and that he will bring people into your life who will love and accept you also.

Father,

The fact that you were rejected and that you understand my loneliness brings me hope. At times I feel like no one understands where I am and how I feel. It helps me to know that you understand what it feels like to be rejected. Thank you that you have chosen me. I pray that I will always walk beside you and trust you. Amen.

REFLECTION QUESTIONS

1. When do you feel the most alone?

2. How does it make you feel to know that Jesus was also rejected?

3. How does knowing that Jesus sees you and has chosen you help you feel?

My Prayer and Reflection

_____

_____

_____

_____

_____

_____

_____

_____

_____

_____

_____

_____

_____

_____

_____

_____

_____

_____

_____

Complete Expression of Love

We know how much God loves us, and we have put our trust in his love.
God is love, and all who live in love live in God, and God lives in them.
1 JOHN 4:16

When we don't give ourselves a lot of love, it's hard to imagine someone else loving us. But there is someone who always loves us no matter what we do. You probably know by now who that someone is. Yep, it's God. He *is* love. He is not against you, but for you. Think about that for just a moment. The God of the Universe, the Creator of all, the almighty, sovereign God, is FOR you. Take that in, and breathe a sigh of relief right now. God does not count your sins against you; you have already been forgiven. Even before you knew who he was, he forgave every bad thing you have ever done or ever will do.

Love like that is hard to comprehend. As hard as it is to understand, we must try. What you believe about God and his love for you affects every part of your life. It affects how secure you are as a young woman, it affects the way you accept love and the way you love others, it affects the view you have of the world around you. If you accept God's love for you, then you will understand you are a daughter of the most high King. If you accept his love for you, you will have a much easier time loving others and giving them grace because you have been given love and grace. The love of God is the most complete expression of love there is, and we are so fortunate to receive this amazing love.

Father,
The love you give is hard to comprehend, but I am working to believe
you at your word. Thank you for your love and your compassion for me.
Thank you for forgiving my sins, even the sins I committed before
I knew you. May I be as loving to others as you are to me. Amen.

REFLECTION QUESTIONS

1. What does it mean to you when someone is *for* you?

2. Being fully loved gives you a clear path to loving others. How can you do a better job of fully loving others?

3. God has made you special! What are some things you love about the way God made you?

❧ My Prayer and Reflection ❧

_____

_____

_____

_____

_____

_____

_____

_____

_____

_____

_____

_____

_____

_____

_____

_____

_____

God Will Fight for You

The L<small>ORD</small> himself will fight for you. Just stay calm.
EXODUS 14:14

Having someone in your corner or on your side makes all the difference in the world. Someone to see your side of the story and fight your enemies for you. Know what? You already have that someone—God is your person. In Exodus, the Israelites were fleeing from four hundred years of being slaves to the Egyptians. The Israelites had left Egypt and were making their way to the land that God had promised them. Originally the Egyptians had let the Israelites go, but after they left, Pharaoh changed his mind and sent his whole army to capture them and bring them back to Egypt. As you can imagine, the Israelites were in fear for their lives. But God answered their prayers in Exodus 14:14 when he said, "I will fight for you." And then he told them to be calm—he had the situation under control.

Let God fight your battles for you. He has the situation under control, and your job is just to stay calm. You don't need to fight back or take matters into your own hands. You don't need to prove your point or fight to be heard. God knows what needs to happen, and he knows exactly what to do. Let God fight for you. Be still. Stay calm. Pray. God is your person!

Father,
What a great story you tell us about the Israelites and how you fought for them. Thank you that your promise still holds true for me. Give me the courage to be still and not take matters into my own hands. Thank you for fighting my battles for me. Amen.

REFLECTION QUESTIONS

1. Are you a fighter, or do you usually sit back and not get engaged? What usually happens as a result of this?

2. What battles are you fighting right now? Is it hard for you to fully trust that God will fight for you? Why or why not?

3. What do you think it would look like if you allowed God to fight your battles for you?

ᥱᥱ My Prayer and Reflection ᥱᥱ

_____

_____

_____

_____

_____

_____

_____

_____

_____

_____

_____

_____

_____

_____

_____

_____

_____

_____

_____

_____

You Have Value

Look at the ravens. They don't plant or harvest or store food in barns, for God feeds them. And you are far more valuable to him than any birds!.
LUKE 12:24

Do you think that you have value? Do you see yourself as someone of importance? Do you ever look in the mirror and say, "I like that girl"? Well, you should! Knowing your value in life will change the way you view life. If you do not feel like you are worth much, then you will be more likely to have a negative view of yourself. You may feel like you are unworthy of certain things. But if you recognize you are a precious, beautiful young lady, both inside and out, then you will hold your head up with a little more confidence, and you will know your value and expect others to follow suit. You will demand to be treated with respect because you know that you deserve to be respected.

Regardless of how you feel about yourself, God places great value on your life. In his sight, you are precious and lovely. Your identity is not in what you do in life, how much you accomplish, who you know, or what you achieve. Your value is cemented in who you are in Christ. You are God's chosen daughter, and he loves you with all his heart. You are a daughter of the King. So hold your head high. If someone talks hatefully or disrespectfully to you, don't accept it. Know in your heart that the things that person says are not true. Demand to be treated better. You deserve it because you are a precious daughter of God. You have value.

Father,

Help me to see myself as you see me. Other people can be hateful sometimes, and their words can bring me down. When that happens, God, remind me that I am precious and worthy of your love. Thank you for loving me and for choosing me to be your daughter. Thank you that you have given me value. Amen.

REFLECTION QUESTIONS

1. Do you feel worthy of God's love? Why or why not?

2. What do you think it means to be a daughter of the most high King?

3. Because you are valuable to God, he will meet all your needs. What are the needs you have right now?
    Physical needs:
    Emotional needs:
    Spiritual needs:
    Relational needs:

My Prayer and Reflection

_____

_____

_____

_____

_____

_____

_____

_____

_____

_____

_____

_____

_____

_____

_____

_____

_____

You Are Beautiful

*To all who mourn in Israel, he will give a crown of beauty
for ashes, a joyous blessing instead of mourning, festive
praise instead of despair. In their righteousness, they will be
like great oaks that the LORD has planted for his own glory.*

ISAIAH 61:3

It's hard to feel beautiful when your face is breaking out from stress, when you compare your (unfiltered) image in the mirror to the (filtered) images on Instagram, when you feel like your personality isn't as fun and bubbly as your best friend's. Sometimes life just feels blah, which makes you feel blah. But God has the ability to take the ashes of your life and turn them into beauty. If you are from a broken home, if you struggle with your body image, if you have depression or anxiety of any sort—anything that makes you feel less than—God can make you whole. He wants you to know that you are his beautiful creation.

Every girl wants to be beautiful—for someone to look at her and to see her value and her worth, for someone to cherish and adore her. God has declared that you are beautiful. He wants to take your sorrow and make you joyful. He wants to take your hopelessness and give you hope—hope in him, and hope for a bright future. If you will trust and believe him today, your walk with him will be strengthened. You will become like an oak tree with deep roots tied to God. And you will be able to look in the mirror and see that you are beautiful!

Father,

*Thank you that you can turn my ashes into beauty, my sorrow
into joy. Thank you that you can give me hope when I have none.
These teen years are hard, and I'm trying to figure them out. I am so
grateful that I'm not alone and that I have you by my side. Amen.*

REFLECTION QUESTIONS

1. When do you feel the most precious and beautiful? What makes you feel this way?

2. What do you place your identity in—your performance, your looks, your talents, your achievements?

3. What happens when you feel like you don't measure up?

4. How does it make you feel to know that God doesn't care about your achievements or anything that the world sees as "beauty," but he accepts you just as you are?

My Prayer and Reflection

_____

_____

_____

_____

_____

_____

_____

_____

_____

_____

_____

_____

_____

_____

You Are Loved

Long ago the L\ord\ said to Israel: "I have loved you, my people, with an everlasting love. With unfailing love I have drawn you to myself."
JEREMIAH 31:3

As you walk the halls in your school, as you step onto the ball field or the cheerleading field, as you enter the theater, the dance studio, or the music room, as you walk into your church or the place where you work, do you feel loved? Do you feel accepted for who you are? Or do you feel like you have to act a certain way or achieve certain things to be included and appreciated? Do you feel like people expect certain things from you, and if you meet their expectations, you will be loved and accepted?

The good news is that God loves and accepts you exactly as you are. And his love lasts forever—so you will be loved forever. To be loved is what we all want and desire. We all want to be accepted as we are and not have to change in order for someone to love us. God accepts you with all your little quirks and goofiness. God accepts your need to be heard, your need to have your own way, and your need to be valued. He knows your "chill" personality and delights in you. He sees your need for perfection and loves that about you. He also sees your fun-loving side, the aspect of your personality that always wants to turn everything into a party. He loves your leadership even though your peers don't appreciate it all the time. You are dearly loved by your heavenly Father. Don't ever forget it.

Father,

I am loved—thank you! I am cherished and adored by you, which makes all the difference in the world. I am never alone, and for that I praise you. Please help me to remember this when I think I have to act a certain way or do certain things to be accepted by others. Thank you that your love lasts forever. Amen.

REFLECTION QUESTIONS

1. On a scale of 1–10, 1 being the lowest and 10 the highest, where do you rate yourself in feeling loved and accepted by your peers? By your parents? By the people in your church?

2. What makes you feel accepted? What makes you not feel accepted?

3. How does it make you feel to know that God loves and accepts you just the way you are? How do you think knowing this can help you love and accept others?

❧ My Prayer and Reflection ❧

_____

_____

_____

_____

_____

_____

_____

_____

_____

_____

_____

_____

_____

_____

_____

_____

_____

_____

_____

God Is Our Comforter

All praise to God, the Father of our Lord Jesus Christ. God is our merciful Father and the source of all comfort. He comforts us in all our troubles so that we can comfort others. When they are troubled, we will be able to give them the same comfort God has given us.
2 CORINTHIANS 1:3–4

We all go through trials and hardships. Life is not perfect, and the teenage years can definitely prove that to be true! Think about all the changes that have happened since you were in elementary school. Have you moved houses or schools? Does your friend group look totally different than it used to? Have you had some not-so-great dating experiences? Have you wondered who exactly you are—and who exactly you are becoming? Even though life is not perfect, God is perfect. That makes him the best one to guide us through life. God will walk with us through any trial we may face. He comforts us when we are sad and brokenhearted. He gives us love and understanding when we are being bullied by other kids. Whether your trial is at home, at school, on the ballfield, or even at church, God is always with you. He is your comforter.

Throughout your life, God will bring other people into your life who may be going through the same situations you've gone through. Come alongside them and comfort them. Point them to God, and help them see that he loves them and will be there for them too. It is a beautiful thing to be able to come alongside another person and say, "I have walked in your shoes. I understand, and this is what helped me." As God comforts you, you can help comfort others.

Father,
Your comfort and love have gotten me through a lot of hard situations. I am so grateful to have you in my life, Lord. Help me to notice when others are suffering as well. Help me to comfort others the way you comfort me. Amen.

REFLECTION QUESTIONS

1. What trials and hardships are you facing right now?

2. How can you see God working in your life as you deal with hard things? How has he helped you with hard things in the past?

3. Is there anyone in your life who is going through a hard time right now? How can you be there for them and help ease their pain?

My Prayer and Reflection

_____

_____

_____

_____

_____

_____

_____

_____

_____

_____

_____

_____

_____

_____

_____

_____

_____

_____

_____

Purposeful Life

You watched me as I was being formed in utter seclusion,
as I was woven together in the dark of the womb. You saw
me before I was born. Every day of my life was recorded in your
book. Every moment was laid out before a single day had passed.

PSALM 139:15–16

Teenage years can be hard years. At times it can feel like the world is against you. Friends can be moody, disloyal, and downright hostile at times. Sometimes you can feel like all you do is disappoint the adults in your life, and you just don't know what everyone wants from you. At times you can look around and think that everyone has a purpose to their life, but what is your purpose? Maybe you don't know what you want to be when you grow up, and maybe sometimes you don't really care. You may think your life has no purpose, no meaning.

The Bible talks about this very thing. We are assured that God saw us even before we were created. God saw you then, and he sees you now. You are not alone, you are not forgotten, you are valuable to him. God has a purpose for your life, and in due time he will reveal it to you. But in the meantime, let your purpose in life be to glorify God in all that you do. Glorify God when you talk to people by making sure the words you speak are uplifting and loving. Glorify God when you play sports by having good sportsmanship and being an encouraging teammate. Glorify God in the work that you do, whether it is school work or chores around your house or a part-time job, by having a positive attitude and doing your best. Glorify God in your relationships by being a good friend who is loyal and loving. Glorify God with your relationships with boys by honoring your body and theirs. Glorify God when you're at home by treating your parents with respect and obeying them. Your life has meaning, and you were created for a reason and a purpose. Live every day to the fullest, live for God, and you will lead a purposeful life.

Father,

Thank you for always seeing me and loving me. It brings
me great joy to know you care about me, that you know the
plan for my life even when I don't. Teach me how to trust in you
and to rest in you. Teach me how to glorify you in all that I do.
I don't think I've ever really thought about glorifying you in
all those simple ways. I love you, Lord; thank you for loving me.

REFLECTION QUESTIONS

1. Do you struggle with the direction your life is going? In what areas do you most struggle?

2. What do you think it means to glorify God in all that you do?

3. What does "live every day to the fullest" mean to you?

4. What do you imagine that a life of purpose would look like?

My Prayer and Reflection

_____

_____

_____

_____

_____

_____

_____

_____

_____

_____

_____

_____

_____

_____

_____

_____

_____

_____

_____

_____

_____

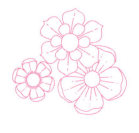